ANTHONY C. SCIRÉ

The Power *of* 2

The Best Way to the Top

Win **BIG** with People in Your Work and in Life

Foreword by Michael Hottinger
A Survivor of the World Trade Center

The Power of 2

ANTHONY C. SCIRÉ

Copyright © 2003 by Anthony C. Sciré
Telephone: (941) 596-4905
motivation@schmoozie.com
www.schmoozie.com

Published by
Possibility Press
posspress@aol.com
www.possibilitypress.com
www.thepowerof2.us
Available to the Book Trade from Ingram and Baker & Taylor

1   2   3   4   5   6   7   8   9   10

Publisher's Cataloging-in-Publication
(Prepared by Quality Books, Inc.)

Sciré, Anthony C.
  The Power of 2: Win BIG with people in your work and in life.
Anthony C. Sciré -- 1st ed.
  LCCN: 2001135267
  ISBN: 0-938716-45-X (cloth)

     1. Success in business. 2. Interpersonal relations.
I. Title.

HF5386.S35 2002   650.1'3
                                                         QB101-201121

For Information About Sharing *The Power of 2*
and Tony Sciré's Speaking and Consulting, See Page 173.

Manufactured in the United States of America

Dedication

This book is dedicated to all those who were lost, injured, or suffered, because of the heinous terrorist attacks of September 11, 2001, as well as those who assisted in the rescue and recovery, and helped in other ways including:

- The people in sales, marketing, and other occupations, from the United States and all over the world, who worked in the World Trade Center—tirelessly building caring relationships every day—and the associates, visitors, and others who were in and around the buildings.
- The people who worked in the Pentagon, unselfishly dedicating themselves to the nation, and the visitors and associates who were with them.
- The four brave and heroic airline crews, and the passengers who were traveling for business, pleasure, or other reasons.
- The brave and heroic firefighters, police officers, healthcare workers, social workers, other public servants, clergy, carpenters, iron workers, construction crews, truck drivers, volunteers, and other people—who unselfishly gave of their time, energy, and for many, even their lives, to save and comfort others and clean up the devastation.
- All the individuals and organizations, throughout the world, who came together to pray, give financial aid, and provide other support.

Those who survived, which really includes all of us, need to continue moving forward with increasing strength, faith, compassion, and resolve. This is the best way for us to ensure that those innocent, hard-working, dedicated people shall not have died, been injured, suffered, or helped in vain.

The horrific events of that fateful day served as a giant wake-up call that life is all too short and precious. Therefore, we all need to spread more *love*—and be *nice, kind,* and *good* to everyone we know or meet, in everything we think, say, and do, as we fully live and contribute each day.

Our thoughts, prayers, and sympathies go out to all, as we honor everyone affected with a stronger commitment to creating world peace. We are deeply saddened at the horrendous losses, yet grateful that the experience has brought and continues to bring our world closer together.

With loving respect and warmest regards,

Tony Sciré
and Possibility Press

Acknowledgment

In appreciation for the many blessings I have received in my personal life and career, all of the net profits after taxes and expenses that I earn from this book will be given to support the charitable needs of others.

First of all, I thank God, our Founding Fathers, and the American people for the privilege to live, raise my family, conduct business, and follow my dream of selling, writing, and speaking, under the flag of diversity, democracy, freedom, and opportunity.

Special thanks and acknowledgment go to St. Jude, who I believe played a major role in this book being published.

Thank you readers, for wanting to make this world a better place by learning about and using the ideas presented in this book—and leading others to do the same. I hope the information shared and the skills and approaches revealed will make a positive difference in the way you build relationships in this high-tech world of ours.

A special thanks goes out to all the wonderful clients and prospects I have had the good fortune of meeting.

A special thanks to the people within my industry who have worked with me over my 27-year career. Each one of you has touched me in your own special way, and you each uniquely personify high-touch relationship building.

A special thanks to my wife, Gail, who believes in me and encouraged me to write this book. Gail, you are truly a remarkable woman. I love you so very much.

A special thanks to my children, Donna and Tony. Over the years you have brought me so much love and joy. I love you.

A special thank you to my mom, Theresa. You are truly the "Queen of High-Touch Relationship Building." I have learned so much about people and life from you.

A special thanks to Dawn Josephson and Dr. Brother Daniel Adams. Your editing has, without a doubt, helped make this book what it is.

A special thanks to the sales support people, coworkers, and customer service agents who worked with me over the years. You and your hard work, both presale and postsale, have played a large part in our success. You are truly appreciated by all the salespeople every day.

And last, but not least, a special thanks to the entire staff at *Possibility Press* for your tremendous editorial and creative contributions. You gave me what I was looking for and have reminded me that anything is possible as long as we have a positive mental attitude, a big dream, and do whatever it takes to make it come true.

Contents

"*Each of us now has a second chance to be the person we were meant to be. Now is truly the time to better define your heartfelt purpose and focus on it.*"

—Mike Hottinger

A Second Chance
to Make a Difference
by Mike Hottinger

September 11, 2001, dawned as a bright and beautiful day, with the sun climbing into a brilliant blue sky. As usual, I went to my office at the World Trade Center (WTC) on the 26th floor of Tower One.

I had just hung up the telephone and began enjoying a cup of tea. All of a sudden, at around 8:45 a.m., the whole office moved violently about a foot to the right, and then back. Everything in the room shook. It felt as though a major earthquake had struck.

I instantly stood up and looked out the windows, only to see all kinds of debris raining down from the sky. Instinctively, I decided to get out of the building. Along with thousands of others, I slowly made my way down the smoke-filled stairs. When I finally reached the plaza level, I looked out in horror to see burning debris in the fountain area.

My inclination was that I was now safe, and I wanted to wait to see who was coming out of the building behind me. But the police insisted that I keep moving. When I finally reached West Street, the police once again pushed me to keep moving. But when I heard the great roar, I stopped and turned around. I then had the shock of my life as I watched in horror as the WTC collapsed! It was as though my whole life was falling apart.

Unfortunately, our reality must often fall apart before we can get it together and become the person God created us to be. It seems as though we must be humbled and brought to our knees. Some sort of crisis needs to enter our lives before most of us are willing to make a change for the good.

This, of course, can happen through illness, divorce, financial challenges, fires, floods, and other difficulties. These events tend to shake us to the core. They make us realize that, for some reason, we are still here. We've survived the crisis or devastation because our work isn't done.

Now consider the police officers and firefighters who risked or sacrificed their lives for us. They selflessly entered those burning buildings to help, and insisted that we keep moving. They, for sure, remind us what caring about others is all about. To ensure that what those brave souls did was not in vain, we all need to seriously think about how we treat others and perhaps make some changes. As a result, their valiant efforts will have benefited humanity in an even more profound way.

In essence, these events give all of us a second chance—a chance to do something better than we've ever done before. They give us a second chance to be better givers and greater lovers of people, as well as the opportunity to make an even bigger difference in the world.

Experiencing the collapse of the WTC firsthand caused me to ask myself some serious questions: Have I loved people well enough and treated them with the respect they deserved? Did I ever say anything unkind to those I worked with and would never see again—for which I failed to apologize and make amends? None of us truly knows whether we will ever see or talk to any particular person ever again. If only for this reason, we all need to love well and be respectful and kind to everyone we encounter. After all, we only live each moment once.

So what was the meaning of September 11th anyway? What lessons can we learn from the horrific events of that fateful day when freedom was attacked?

Can we, the civilized peoples of the world, make planet Earth a better place by being *nice, kind,* and *good* to everyone we know and meet? Yes! We can all recognize that each of us now has a second chance to be the person we were meant to be. Now is truly the time to better define your heartfelt purpose and focus on it. Remember, as it says in the Bible, "You reap what you sow."

Tony Sciré has been my dear friend for many years, and I consider him to be one of the finest, most caring, and successful relationship builders in the world. I am here to tell you that reading *The Power of 2* can be the launching pad for a new beginning in creating the fine relationships you've always wanted—in all areas of your life. In doing so, you will be happier and find yourself reaching your goals and objectives, and making your dreams come true.

Tony is a lover of people extraordinaire. Through this book, he shares how he treats others all around the world. You will learn how he succeeded as an international businessman by caring about others and helping them achieve their goals.

Would you like a second chance at life like the one that's been given to me? Well, here it is and now's the time! Read and apply the principles in this magnificent book and go forward living your life—with more passion and love for others than ever before.

We're all in this together. Let's seize the moment and make each day count by building more caring relationships with each other.

With warm and loving regards,

Mike Hottinger

"One positive dream is more powerful than a thousand negative realities."

—Tony Sciré

The Social Mission of This Book

My dream is to expand the *wonderful wave of kindness* that began on September 11, 2001. The result is this book, which actively recognizes that we all have the responsibility to be *nice, kind,* and *good* to one another. Life is much too short and too precious to be otherwise. And ever since I personally witnessed the devastation of the World Trade Center, I have come to realize that, as individuals throughout the world, we all need to take this responsibility more seriously. Maintain a positive attitude and treat each other in a compassionate, uplifting, respectful manner.

So what is the measure of a person's life anyway? Is it how long we live, how much money we earn, how many things we acquire, or how aggressive we are? Or is it how *nice, kind,* and *good* we are toward others, and the difference we make in the world by helping them improve their lives?

During the days and weeks following September 11, 2001, I experienced how wonderful people were to each other. My objective is to build on that momentum. My hope is that this book will help people all over the world build better relationships to improve the quality of life we all deserve. Always remember, one positive dream is more powerful than a thousand negative realities! Each of us has the *power in the hour* to create a positive attitude and a compassionate state of mind. We can overcome negative influences and make this a better world.

The Power of 2 gives you continuing encouragement to be *nice, kind,* and *good* to everyone you know and meet. That may have sounded foreign or even corny before, but it certainly doesn't anymore. And guess what? *It works!* After all, people are people and everyone has feelings and a heart.

Everyone wants to know how much you care—*about them*—before they care about you and what you know about what you're offering or doing.

Contrary to what you may have been taught or led to believe, being manipulative, intimidating, and aggressive is *not* the best way to the top. It alienates, builds resentment, and drives people away. It's not the way to have great relationships, build a business, succeed on the job or in school, increase sales, contribute to the community, or live a happy life.

You don't need to work, associate, do business with, or sell to strangers ever again. Build rapport with the people you know and meet, by caring about them and being a friend. When people are friends, it's easier and more pleasant to work and do other things together. May the heartfelt, unifying spirit of the high-touch approach to building relationships help all of us strengthen our bonds with everyone.

Now go forward in whatever you are doing, and do it with more resolve, passion, and love than ever before. Always bring out the best in yourself and others. Be appreciative. Thank and compliment people more often to show them you care, as well as to help build their confidence. As the philosopher Goethe said, "Kindness is the golden chain by which society is bound together." Let's make all of our relationships better than they have ever been before. Our communities, schools, workplaces, and other environments will then be kinder, gentler places to be.

The Pledge of
a Loving, Caring Attitude

As you embark on the next stage of your journey, think of *The Power of 2* as your personal coach. If you get lonely, seek its friendship. If you feel a drop in self-confidence, flip through its pages and read a paragraph or two. But above all, believe that you have the power to love and be loved and— *pledge to be nice, kind, and good to everyone you know and meet.*

Now open your mind and heart as you begin reading this book, and start incorporating its message into your life. Let's make this world a better place in which to live, grow, work, and play, and we all will have truly made a difference.

What Is a *High-Touch* Relationship?

A high-touch relationship is a strong, mutually beneficial association of two people who are *nice, kind,* and *good* to each other as they do things together. This is the essence of *The Power of 2.* It begins with a loving, caring attitude toward others, while showing honest concern for their welfare, and keeping in touch.

High-touch relationships are built by touching the hearts of the people you know and meet in your efforts to truly help them. It's going beyond just requirements, facts, and figures. You relate to each person as someone of inherent value. You have a sincere commitment to make a difference, and do whatever it takes to help others win. This goes beyond just fulfilling your role or job description, or conducting everyday activities. You create relationships that become genuine and special friendships.

A high-touch relationship involves being a friend. You then help that friend solve his or her problems to achieve a worthy dream, goal, or objective, while overcoming challenges along the way. It is also being of additional assistance, as needed. As friends, you become partners in success—working together as a team to benefit yourselves and others. It's friends taking care of friends.

High-touch relationships come out of loving whatever you do. They are nurtured by taking an interest in and having compassion for the people you are working and associating with, and putting your heart and soul into all of it. You create and maintain true emotional connections, becoming kindred in spirit and heart.

High-touch relationship builders are friendly, caring, fun loving, respectful, creative, honest, appreciative, humble, patient, other-centered, giving, generous, and empathetic.

Your success, especially in today's high-tech world, depends largely on your ability to meet, understand, be concerned about, get along with, and be of service to others. Become a high-touch relationship builder and watch your success and happiness grow. It will positively affect your job, business, or profession, and other activities. The results may astound you and will lead to a gentler, kinder community, workplace, and world. On top of that, your personal relationships and life will improve as well.

"There is no such thing as a self-made person. We are made up of thousands of others. Everyone who has ever done a kind deed for us, or spoken one word of encouragement to us, has entered into the make-up of our character and of our thoughts, as well as our success."

—George Matthew Adams

Is It Possible to
Succeed Alone?

*"The Power of 2 gives you the edge in meeting new people.
It helps you build great relationships in your job, business, or
profession, as well as in your community and personal life."*
—Tony Sciré—

Allow me to introduce myself. I am Tony Sciré, and it is a pleasure to speak with you today through the words in this book.

Would you agree with the following statements? No one can ever benefit in any environment or endeavor until at least two people get together or communicate. To do that most effectively, they need to either have a relationship or start building one. One of them needs to present his or her idea, knowledge, solution, product, service, or opportunity to the other. Finally, they both need to work together to overcome the challenges encountered along the way—to make things happen and get mutually beneficial results.

That's what *The Power of 2* is all about. You'll learn how to meet more people, build finer relationships, and better nurture the ones you already have. This will enable you to more easily reach your goals and objectives, increase your income, and realize your fondest dreams.

I invite you to take a journey with me through the pages of this book. It will expand your vision of how you can build more productive and enjoyable relationships. You'll also learn other skills and approaches to accelerate your success.

People want to work, do business, and associate with those they know, like, trust, and can call friends. This is even truer in today's fast-paced, highly competitive, high-tech times.

Technology provides us with great communication tools. But no matter how sophisticated these tools become, human nature remains the same.

We all need to know someone cares about us and our challenges. The more high-tech our world becomes, the more important it is to build high-touch relationships. This will increase our productivity and help us achieve what we desire.

You may wonder about the title of this book. As it evolved, various titles were considered and test-marketed with key businesspeople. But the final title emerged only after I had some brainstorming sessions with my publisher, and we found ourselves getting closer to finalizing the text. Then, one day, after he had a discussion about the title with one of his largest corporate clients, I received an exciting call from him. He said, "Tony, I think we've finally got the title—it's *The Power of 2*."

Near the middle of the book, there's a discussion about an approach I call *The Power of 2* business card technique, which you can use to expand your sphere of influence. That was it. Eureka! It became crystal clear to us that the power of two people doing things together was the essence of the book. It takes at least two people to communicate, build a relationship, work together, close a deal, or make an agreement or association. It all begins with *The Power of 2*.

Here is an example of how *The Power of 2* works mathematically. Suppose you were offered the choice of having either $500,000 right now—tax free—or a penny doubled every day for a month. Which would you take? If you took the $500,000 instead of the penny, you would have made a big mistake. However, if you took the penny, you would be $5,368,709.12 richer by day 30! You would have more than ten times the lump sum cash offer—all because you believed in *The Power of 2*.

To illustrate the importance of *The Power of 2* in sharing what you're doing with others, ask yourself this: What would have happened if Thomas Edison had stayed in his lab and never told anyone he had invented the lightbulb? No one would have benefited from his genius or incredible dedication to creating solutions.

I can teach you how to excel in any activity. But I can't teach you how to do it alone! You need at least one other person before anything much can be made to happen. The more people you build high-touch relationships with, the more successful you can become.

My 27-year career has been focused on sales, sales management, and being a vice president for a major international company. I interacted and built relationships with people who were not in sales, as well as those who were. This included people both in and out of our various corporate offices, as well as prospects' and clients' offices throughout the United States, and in many foreign countries. Wherever I went, I used the principles of *The Power of 2,* which are based on being *nice, kind,* and *good* to everyone you know and meet. They are just as applicable in the office or workplace as they are in the field—and wherever else you encounter people.

A major problem in business and community today is that many people are verbally beaten up, disrespected, taken advantage of, and abused. People are lashing out at one another because of their own elevated levels of stress, and lack of skills in building and nurturing relationships.

Whatever roles you may play in your work and in life, you like to be treated in a kind and gentle way. Right? And everyone you come in contact with feels the same. This includes any bosses, coworkers, associates, prospects, and clients you may have. It also consists of those who serve you, your company or organization, and your community. For example, vendors, consultants, service people, freelancers, cleaning people, government employees, and all repair and delivery people like to be treated nicely too.

You cannot function properly in your job, business, or profession, or in the other aspects of your life, without the involvement of others. Everyone you associate or deal with is a part of your "team," and each one plays a role in your success and happiness.

Remember, we all have feelings and long to be appreciated. For example, just imagine how messy, smelly, and unhealthy it would become if your garbage was not picked up regularly. The people who do that are very important to the quality of our lives, and they like to be appreciated too.

In addition to everyone in the workplace, those outside of it need to be treated well too. Build goodwill with everyone, everywhere you go, all the time. You represent not only any company or organization you're with, but yourself, your family, and your community as well. So be generous with your smile☺. Don't give it just to those you would like to work or associate with, or have buy from you. Smile☺ at everyone you know and meet.

Whenever someone asks, "How are you?" always respond in a positive, uplifting way. You could simply say something like, "Great!" even if you don't feel that way. It will actually help you feel better and potentially lead to the start of a new relationship. If you are negative and looking for sympathy, nobody will want to be around you.

Remember, also, that friends care about each other, and a stranger is just a friend you haven't yet met. Make more friends in every arena you're in, and your success will be accelerated in all areas of your life. You can't have great work or life experiences unless you and the people you interact with treat each other in kind and gentle ways—with caring spirits and hearts.

Now, if you're in business or sales, understand that some of your competitors may be able to deliver a product or service, or present an idea or opportunity as well as you can. Some of them may even have a higher profit margin and offer a lower price—just to get the sale. Also understand that people are likely to demand that your product or service be of the highest quality at the lowest price, and include the latest features and benefits.

Today, I challenge you to have the courage to step outside your comfort zones. Do you believe it is a mistake to build friendships with coworkers and associates, as well as with anyone to whom you may sell? If so, the proven ideas presented here can help you develop new comfort zones. Start making more friends and rise to levels of success which you may never have imagined.

I encourage you to keep an open mind so you'll be receptive to some new ideas. Will you stretch beyond your comfort zones today—and every day from now on—and start caring more about people than you ever have before?

I urge you to think about the possibility of reinventing yourself and the way you approach your relationships with the people you work with, lead, and serve. As you master the necessary skills, your relationship-building abilities will improve. Furthermore, networking—meeting new people to build more win-win relationships—will become second nature to you, as well as being a lot of fun!

You may need to increase your sphere of influence. Or you might be just starting a new job, business, profession, or role in the community. In any case, whether you will be networking a little or a lot, the tips, techniques, and approaches you are about to discover will be of great benefit to you. You will also read several true stories from my career experiences to help you apply what you are learning.

With great pleasure, I'll share with you some ideas for getting results with those people who never seem to want to communicate or meet with you. They are the indifferent ones who rarely or never take or return your calls, nor respond to faxes, voicemails, e-mails, or letters. Yes, you are not the only one who experiences that—*by far!*

The ideas in this book are simple, yet powerful. They are based on my experiences in building lasting relationships with all kinds of people, all over the world. This has afforded me the success I now enjoy with clients, coworkers, associates, and others who have become friends. As American statesman John Hay said, "Friends are the sunshine of life."

Some of the skills and approaches I use and present here are based on knocking on doors, cold calling, making phone calls, and going through the nos to find the next yes. I never gave up, quit, or stayed in the office because I didn't want to face another no. I just got out there and did it. That's what you need to do too. Yes, be focused. But don't be pushy or overdo it when meeting and talking with people.

When people are networking at a breakfast or similar venue, they often tend to be obvious about what they want. However, this isn't necessarily the best way to approach starting new relationships.

The best way to meet and get to know new people is simply to chat, speak, or converse with them in a light, easy, informal manner. This may or may not lead to sales, associations, or agreements, but no matter how these encounters turn out, that's okay. If they say no now, they may say yes later. So keep going. For the more successful among us, as well as for those who are truly striving to excel, this approach works.

When you meet, greet, and talk with people, be sure to learn, remember, and use their names. As Dale Carnegie said, "The sweetest sound to people is hearing their own name." It's so true. Most of us like to hear our name while being treated with kindness and consideration. We may not even realize what is actually happening, but it certainly feels good.

If you are in sales, do you remember the last time you called a client or prospect, only to learn that he or she was meeting with a competitor? What do you suppose was happening? They were probably using *The Power of 2,* building a relationship. While you were in the office, at your company, or at home, your competition was out making it happen. They could have taken your client's business or won a mutual prospect's new business. If you don't consistently build and maintain relationships with prospects and clients, your competition could win their business.

As you begin caring more about others, the easier it will be to understand and get along with them. It will also become more of a natural, fun thing to do. Building great relationships will become the norm for you. As a result, you are likely to find that more people will want to work, associate, or do business with you.

Anyone can make an acquaintance for a day. However, the high performers—those who are consistently reaching or exceeding their goals—build long-term, high-touch relationships. So, to win BIG with people, that's what you need to do too.

When you apply the ideas in this book, you will set yourself apart. Those you interact with will feel as if they've been embraced by *a wonderful wave of kindness*. You'll be known as a caring person who goes out of his or her way to do the extra things most others won't bother doing.

I have built high-touch relationships with people in practically every country of the world. No matter where I went, though, I always found that using high-tech communication devices never replaced interpersonal interactions. Since they provide only low-touch capabilities, they simply can't convey the warmth of a human being. Therefore, having interpersonal interactions is key to building high-touch relationships. This will give you the edge over those who don't. From now on, you can excel to higher levels when it comes to meeting new people, and building and maintaining harmonious, productive relationships.

As Plautus said, "Your wealth is where your friends are." And as Malcolm Forbes noted, "Contrary to the old cliché, genuinely nice people most often *do* finish first or very near it."

Now, more than ever before, let's be *nice, kind,* and *good* to everyone we know and meet. Let's make more new friends and finish first more often. Start using the principles and approaches in *The Power of 2,* and build high-touch relationships to win BIG with people. You'll accelerate your success in your work, community, and personal life, and accomplish more of your dreams, goals, and objectives.

All the best and God bless,

"We all need to know someone cares about us and our challenges. The more high-tech our world becomes, the more important it is to build high-touch relationships. This will increase our productivity and help us achieve what we desire."

—Tony Sciré

"'Tis the human touch in the world that counts—the touch of your hand and mine—which means far more to the sinking heart than shelter, bread, or wine. For shelter is gone when the night is o'er, and bread lasts only a day. But the touch of the hand and the sound of the voice live on in the soul always."

—Spencer M. Free

–1–

Use Your People Power to Enhance Your Ability to Better Relate in an Increasingly High-Tech World

*"As our world becomes more high-tech, we need to build
more high-touch relationships. The more technology we use, the
more people need to know others care about them."*
—Tony Sciré—

People power has been around for centuries—at least since biblical times. Our ancestors undoubtedly used their people power as well—and to the best of their abilities—to get the cooperation they wanted! Your parents and siblings used it, too, when they wanted you to do something, even though neither you nor they may have been aware of it.

So what is people power? It's consciously being other-centered in building mutually beneficial relationships. This means taking your eyes off yourself so you can connect with others. It's sincerely focusing on and caring about others, as you assist them in whatever way you can.

Consider the power of charisma. Some people seem to just naturally have it, while others obviously don't. Why is it that a room lights up when someone with charisma walks in? Why do some people easily attract others, while the majority seem to have a difficult time of it? Are those with charisma simply born with it, or is it something they developed along the way?

While some people seem to be born with a lot of charisma, most everyone has it to one degree or another. The great news is anyone can develop it to a higher level! Start by identifying someone with charisma—like a favorite boss, mentor, leader, or friend—and observe their interactions with others. Then ask them for some suggestions of how you, too, can develop your charisma.

Build relationships by creating a *people-power process*—a high-touch approach that can be used by everyone in every circumstance. For example, think back to your first day of school. As you sat at your desk while the teacher stood in front of the room, there was probably a time when the two of you had at least brief eye contact. That was the teacher's people-power process in action. He or she endeavored to connect with you so you would feel welcomed.

Do you remember the last time you said hello to someone you didn't know? How about the first time you stood up and made a presentation to a group of people you had never met before? Perhaps you have been involved with a social organization where you raised money or talked to people about an upcoming event. As a college student, you may have pledged to join a fraternity or sorority. If you are a parent, you've undoubtedly asked a son or daughter to do something. Each of the above situations begs the use of a people-power process.

We all use a people-power process when we build relationships. In fact, this observation served as the foundation for creating *The Power of 2*. We will always continue to develop our relationships based on our ability to use our people power, take action, and build rapport. As the world becomes more high-tech, people need to build more high-touch relationships. The more technology we use, the more people need to know others care about them.

Three Key Components for Initiating Relationships

Whenever you meet someone with whom you want to build a long-lasting relationship, employ the following three components: release your people power through your eyes; make verbal contact; and develop harmony.

First—*Release Your People Power Through Your Eyes.* Your eyes help you communicate your emotions. Two people making sincere eye contact can connect emotionally. This is essential to the beginning of all successful relationships, and it can help you build trust right from the start.

Second—*Make Verbal Contact.* Say a cheerful hi, hello, good morning, or something similar. This is general courtesy, and it can "break the ice" and serve as the catalyst for starting a conversation. It's easy to do, and it can help brighten someone else's day, as well as your own.

Men, think back to the first time you saw a woman you wanted to meet, and just knew you needed to make the first move with a friendly hello. And ladies, recall the first time you saw a man you wanted to meet, and felt compelled to initiate a conversation. What was that experience like for you? Did you take action or not?

Making initial verbal contact is essential to people-power processing. The way you greet someone can make all the difference in the world. It could be key in determining whether or not a relationship evolves. If so, it may even affect how long it will last. No matter what you do, though, always be friendly and considerate of others.

Third—*Develop Harmony.* The dictionary defines harmony as—"being in agreement in action, ideas, sense, feeling; friendly relations." Harmony needs to be established before much of anything can be accomplished with anyone else.

If a relationship never gets off the ground or an endeavor fails, it's usually due to a lack of action or incompatibility. Harmony was never developed or maintained. Developing harmony with others, to at least some degree, is necessary before they'll say yes to what you're suggesting. The desire to create mutually beneficial relationships sets the stage for harmony to begin.

People-power processing applies to anyone who wants to connect and build relationships. And it's becoming even more essential in our increasingly high-tech environment. Technology is wonderful, but it simply can't, won't, and doesn't care about others. That's left for us people to do! So the time to use your people power is *now*—more than ever.

Why Is Your People Power Important?

People power is the foundation for building superb relationships with all kinds of people in every area of life. Using it can help you unlock the door to achieving your objectives, as you help others achieve theirs.

You may think of ultimate people power as the ability to know and work with influential people in high places. But that's just part of it. It is also recognizing and using your inborn people power to develop more and better win-win relationships with people at all levels.

Some of the people-power components you can use to build great relationships are your:

- Smile☺
- Kind words
- Eye contact
- Tone of voice
- Posture
- Interest
- Conversation
- Creativity
- Facial expressions
- Attention

- Balance
- Sensitivity
- Keeping in touch
- Pleasant demeanor
- Graciousness
- Positive attitude
- Humility
- Patience
- Body movements
- Gratitude

Master the skill of using your people power. Develop its readily accessible components, and you can dramatically increase your ability to create more top-notch relationships. And always use your people power to help others—never to manipulate them. As former United States President George H. W. Bush said, "Use power to help people. For we are given power not to advance our own purposes, nor to make a great show in the world, nor a name. There is but one just use of power, and it is to serve people."

Understanding How Your People Power Works

Your people power works the best when you believe in yourself and the fine qualities you have to give others. Your smile, kind words, eye contact, and pleasant demeanor can positively affect the direction of your conversations. If you don't use your people power, you will negatively affect your conversations.

For example, I have observed some salespeople dominate conversations. They were so overpoweringly aggressive—oblivious to other people's wants, needs, and feelings—that their clients or prospects became very uncomfortable. Sometimes, I could feel the tension growing between them. I wanted to jump in and defuse the various situations before there was a breakdown in communications.

I have always enjoyed watching the best salespeople in action. They gently and kindly navigate conversations by using their people power to connect. They created an atmosphere where their clients or prospects felt comfortable and important, both throughout and after the communication. Do the same, and you'll develop more high-quality relationships in all areas of your life.

To help create a people-power process, feed yourself positive thoughts everywhere you go. Negative thoughts inhibit the process from ever getting started. As we'll discuss in the next chapter, *your attitude can get you gratitude.*

Would you agree with that? Would you also agree that a positive attitude can help you get more out of life than a negative attitude ever could?

Accept these ideas today and begin a new growth process. Start integrating people power into your thinking. This will help you have an exciting new perspective on building relationships. Use the following approach to help eliminate any excuses or concerns about failure.

How Is the People-Power Process Built?

During my extensive career, I have learned that people generally do not fail because their relationships ended. They typically fail simply because they never even got their relationships started. They don't initiate conversations, make the necessary calls, schedule appointments, or follow up. They never *really* began the relationships!

Remember, people-power processing always involves being other-centered. Getting to the next step with someone requires taking action, while harnessing and using your people power with *integrity*. Then, as you build rapport, you pave the way for open, honest, harmonious communication. Observe and understand the other person's style and personality, and act accordingly. You are "tuning in" to that individual.

People-power processing can help you take relationships from ideas to living realities. Incorporate the following three building blocks into your relationship-building efforts: recognize your people power as a resource and tremendous ally; take action with it; and use it to build rapport.

First—*Recognize Your People Power as a Resource and Tremendous Ally.* Previously, we spoke about charisma and how anyone can develop it. Again, observe those you admire who have it, learn from them, and adapt it as a part of your own behavior. Use your charisma. It will help you create win-win relationships to accomplish mutual goals.

You were born with a seed of greatness—that's a given. As you grow that seed and develop its strength, it gives you the positive, magnetic people power you need to succeed in a really big way. Use that power to drive your dreams and objectives into reality. Other people can sense your invigorating energy and enthusiasm when you are talking with them. It's contagious!

Remember, people don't fail because they never get a chance at building relationships. They fail because they kill the spirit inside themselves—the one that drives them to succeed with others. I have seen many people fail simply because they destroyed their own driving force to persevere and follow through.

I remember one very good salesperson who came into my office angry, disgusted, and ready to quit. He was not making his quota that month. Every sales call had ended in rejection. Many of the people he was scheduled to meet with were canceling their appointments. He had let his fire for desire dwindle, killing his spirit to succeed. His people power became weak, and he needed encouragement.

I quickly told him to sit down and relax. "You are *not* quitting or giving up!" I said. "You are better than that!" I repeated those words over and over—until his eyes began to shine again. The glimmer returned, and I knew he was getting his spirit back.

Sometimes, all we need are a few encouraging words. This builds our self-belief so we can get back on track and moving forward again.

Have you allowed your spirit to weaken or die? If so, it's time to remember some past successes. This will help you get reenergized.

Here's a step-by-step process for rebuilding your spirit:

1. Get back to basics—B2B. Discover what you're not doing that you need to do, and go do it.

2. Take full advantage of continuing educational and motivational materials and opportunities. This could include books, tapes, videos, CDs, seminars, product/service fairs, and trade shows.
3. Get out and meet more people.
4. Make more calls.
5. Set more appointments.
6. Make more presentations.
7. Create opportunities. Don't expect them to come to you. Be proactive—*initiate the action and make things happen!*

If you ever lose your spirit or burn out, don't worry. Negative energy may have pulled you down, but positive energy can bring you back up again—every time! As Ralph Waldo Emerson said, "Our greatest glory doesn't consist of never failing, but in rising every time we fall."

Second—*Take Action by Using Your People Power.* When you take action, you are shaping your destiny. All the power and resources in the world are meaningless, unless you take appropriate action. As the saying goes, "Actions speak louder than words."

Awake each day believing you have more chances to do what you had planned to do yesterday but didn't. You are alive with opportunities. You are ready to seize the day and reach for your goals. *Your past does not determine your future.* What happened yesterday is history—you can't change it. Leave it back there where it belongs. Learn from it, and use that knowledge to reenergize and carry yourself into a new day.

Start using your people power to more effectively reach your goals. Arm yourself with this valuable and cherished tool to alter your path or create a new destiny. Consistently take the necessary action, one step at a time, and you'll find yourself developing new and different results. You'll be filled with hope. The future you want already belongs to you. Go ahead and claim it!

Take people-power action to get and stay excited. It will move you to the next level in building high-touch relationships. Always communicate positive, uplifting messages to yourself. Say something like, "I'm excited and I can do it!" This attitude enhances your ability to build the relationships you would love to have.

Third—*Build Rapport by Using Your People Power.* Rapport is the passkey which opens many doors for achieving success with others. It unlocks your people power and enables you to generate magic in your communications. Rapport is typically thought of as two people talking and building a harmonious relationship. But remember, to have outstanding communications, *you* need to take the lead. Depending on other people to take the initiative generally leads to disappointment.

To start developing rapport, you first need to communicate positive thoughts enthusiastically. This sets the stage for you to take the action necessary to get to the next step in building relationships. It will help you build the confidence you need when meeting new people, so you can start relationships with them.

Rapport is the building block that drives a high-touch relationship. Be sensitive to the emotions of the person you are endeavoring to get to know and understand. When building rapport, you are establishing an emotional bond. This can be done most effectively when you "tune in" to the emotional "station" on which the other person is "broadcasting."

Your communications consist of three facets—content, tone, and posture:

1. Content—What are you saying?
2. Tone—How do you sound to other people?
3. Posture—How do you look to other people? What are your eyes, facial expressions, and other body positions and movements saying? Are they congruent with what

you are communicating, in the words you use and by
the tone of your voice?

The key to relating to someone, when building rapport,
is understanding that person's emotional needs. Part of
that can be accomplished by building compatibility between the two of you. For example, when you meet
someone who is low-key and soft-spoken, be low-key and
soft-spoken yourself. If you are loud and too enthusiastic,
he or she may feel uncomfortable. You could lose his or
her interest. If, on the other hand, that person is loud and
you are soft-spoken, speak with enthusiasm and more vol-
ume. I call this *blending*.

Blending while building rapport is similar to being like a
mirror. When first getting to know someone, talk, act, sit,
and move in a way that is reflective of the other person's
behavior. Be sensitive to what he or she says and does.
This helps that person feel more comfortable being with
you. You're building relatability by creating a comfort
zone for the other person.

This does not mean you are oblivious to your own natural body movements and personality. In fact, you need to
genuinely be yourself. If you put on a false front, trying to
present an image of somebody you're not, you're being
dishonest. You'll lose the other person's respect and interest. Blend in a way that is natural and relaxed. It's the best
way to build rapport.

Be aware of your own personality and behavioral tendencies and how they might affect others. You may need to
change some of your thinking and balance your behavioral
tendencies in order to build better rapport. This is all a part of
personal growth, which includes learning from others as well
as from your own experiences.

Blending with another person can really help you get into
the feeling and flow of your conversational exchanges. Once

a conversation gets up and running, it will take on a life of its own. You'll be in an emotional stride—giving and receiving ideas—and you'll both become even more relaxed in the process. If you sense you are getting disjointed in your communication, and start feeling awkward, begin blending again to get back in sync with that person.

A key step in building rapport with others begins by blending with *yourself.* Use your people-power components, such as your smile and kind words, with yourself too! Always have a positive attitude about yourself. Let go of any negative experiences or attitudes when you are about to see or work with someone. Then *focus on him or her.*

For example, let's say you just had an argument with someone. Your posture and tonality are probably not going to blend very well with the next person you talk to. You won't be in sync with that person, and he or she will quickly feel you are out of it. Being upset, you are likely to communicate anger and a sense of doubt in an "I-can't-do-it, it-won't-work, I-don't-care-about-you" attitude. This sets the stage for a negative reaction. It's the power of influence— negative influence. This, of course, won't give you the results you want.

Instead of letting a negative attitude ruin your next conversation, take some time to calm yourself down. Before you talk with anyone else, apologize to the person you just argued with—even if it's just for raising your voice. This will help you and that person feel better, whether or not you agree on the issue. It will also free your mind and heart so you can focus on the next person. You can then go forward with the confidence that you'll be more likely to elicit a positive response. Adopt an "I-can-do-it, it-will-work, I-care-about-you" attitude.

Encourage positive feelings in others, by conveying positive messages:

- Maintain plenty of eye contact.

- Wear happy☺ facial expressions, even when you're on the phone!
- Speak in a pleasant tone of voice.
- Have an open, friendly body posture and make gentle movements. Never point a finger at them or cross your arms, even if that's what they do. These negative gestures could create a stand-off.
- Use uplifting words.

You may need to give yourself a positive talking-to before you are able to do all of this effectively—especially if you just had a negative experience. Focus on something positive—something you feel good about every time you remember it. Lift yourself up. Think about your dream or goal, an award or gift you received, a compliment someone gave you, or how much you love your family.

Get into genuine self-rapport by giving yourself positive messages that reinforce the actions you're about to take. Many people don't build great relationships, because they aren't even in rapport with themselves. Rather than accepting and embracing their own ability to do great things, they dump negative ideas on themselves through negative self-talk. They often don't like themselves, which is reflected in all they say and do. Other people tend to notice and respond to that in a negative way.

If you reject yourself and your ideas, how could you possibly expect others to do any differently? What you give to others is what you'll most likely get back.

Failing in almost any arena, including children getting poor grades, can be based on this same idea—people are out of rapport with themselves and their goals. Whether you communicate a positive or negative message to your mind, it will produce the results you request. As Henry Ford said, "If you think you can or you think you can't, you're right."

Use people power with yourself to create positive results! Creating positive relationships with others begins by creating a positive relationship *with yourself.*

The key to building self-rapport is to develop harmony with and belief in yourself. As mentioned earlier, Dale Carnegie observed that the sweetest sound anyone can hear is the sound of his or her own name. And as Carnegie also shared, "Learn to like your own name so others can do the same." Do this, and you'll be better able to focus on them. Get beyond yourself and your own personal challenges. This will enable you to reach out to others and develop the high-touch relationships you need to succeed.

Here are some clues to help you learn to better accept and like yourself so you can enhance your self-rapport:

- Be authentically who you are and don't try to fake people out.
- Pay attention to and courageously express your wants and needs—to yourself and others.

Always show others you care about them. This helps you feel better about yourself and, in turn, builds your self-rapport. After all, most people don't care how much you know until they know how much you care—*about them!*

When you tell yourself to move a finger, it moves. Doesn't it? It is the same way with your attitude. Positive communication with yourself moves your internal voice to produce high energy and greater self-respect. You are building rapport with yourself, which helps you create a solid foundation for building rapport with others.

Carnegie had another big secret in successfully relating with others. The best way to lead others into doing something is to get them to the point where they *want* to do it. Since being self-directed is a basic human desire, building rapport with others gives you the best opportunity to discover what they want. They will then be more receptive to learning how you can help them get it.

Be a Good Listener

Many times when two people first meet, all they do is talk about themselves. They may both get so caught up and self-absorbed that they pay little or no attention to each other.

People like to talk about themselves. So, when you first meet someone, use your people power and *let that person talk!* He or she will love it. Simply start out by asking a question or two, such as, "What do you do for a living?" or "I've never seen you before. How long have you lived in this area?" or "What do you enjoy doing?" You could also pay that person a sincere compliment by noticing what he or she is wearing. You could say, "That's really a sharp suit," or "What a beautiful pin!"

Questions and compliments can make it more comfortable for people to open up to you. You'll be amazed at how much you can learn about them—often in a very short time. Those who don't take the time to listen to others will only get poor results in their relationship-building efforts.

When you meet someone new, let that person "clean" his or her "slate" off first; then you can go in and "write" on it. Give the time and attention he or she may so sorely want and need, and you'll be on your way to making a friend. Most people are starving for attention. Even if you don't say much, others will think you're nice to talk to—because you listened to them.

You may be surprised at how quickly your positive listening to others can lead to their saying yes to what you would like them to do. The key is to be interested in others and allow them to tell you exactly what *they* want. They will then be more likely to be interested in you and what you have to say or offer.

Remember, a positive contact could lead someone into doing something with or buying something from you—and then again, it may not. Your integrity might, instead, lead you to refer him or her to another source that could better meet his or her particular needs. Yes, of course, have the attitude that you would prefer that this person buy from or associate with you—but don't be attached to it. Want what is truly best for that individual. This shows you really care, and you'll feel good about yourself for having done so.

Be assured that, as the saying goes, "What goes around comes around." You will always be rewarded in some way for the help you give others. It may show up sooner or later as a referral, or in some kind words they say about you. Who knows? Even if they say no now, they may say yes later! Furthermore, the benefit you receive may even come from a completely unexpected source. But no matter what happens, always use your people power. It will help you build great high-touch relationships.

"*Gratitude takes three forms: a feeling in the heart, an expression in words, and a giving in return.*"

—John Wanamaker

–2–

Your Attitude Can
Get You Gratitude

*"Have a caring, attentive attitude toward others,
and understand that everyone enjoys a nice
conversation and a bit of fun. This is essential for
you to succeed with people."*
—Tony Sciré—

Whenever you communicate with others, your attitude is key to your success. Maintain a positive attitude, and you'll increase the chances of getting the results you want in all areas of your life.

No matter what you do for a living, or in addition to it, always think of yourself as owning your own business—as being self-employed. You, and you alone, are responsible for your own motivation and success. No one else can reach your objectives for you. If you blame others and your environment, you would only be deluding yourself and diminishing the energy you have available for the task at hand.

Fortify your attitude every day. Associate with positive people, read at least 15 to 20 minutes from an uplifting book, and listen to one or more motivational or educational tapes. And be sure to stay away from negative people. This will help you motivate yourself to do what you need to do—every single day.

Action Is Motion in Process

Start taking action by moving ideas from dreams or objectives to goals on paper. This begins the positive momentum you need to make things happen. For example, tell yourself to take a particular action with a self-rapport statement like, "I'm going to meet and talk with two or more new people today." Your focused energy and a positive attitude can get you gratitude in the form of potential new relationships.

For instance, if you're in sales, the more people you meet and follow up with, the more prospects you'll have. Show how you can help them overcome their challenges with whatever you have to offer, and they may show you gratitude in one form or another. They may become clients or associates, or give you referrals.

In today's fast-paced world, there are many potential distractions. It requires concentrated effort to stay on course. For example, nearly everyone, myself included, has some mood swings. But I don't let them get me down or off track from my goals. My attitude is, *I'm up or I'm getting up!* If I get knocked down, I pick myself up, dust myself off, and get moving again. And you need to do the same. Only then can you swing the door wide open to take full advantage of the opportunities available to help you accomplish your goals.

Turning an Obstacle into an Opportunity—*Flip and Turn*

You can't afford to wait for other people's attitudes to be exactly right for you to make sales, associations, or agreements. You may need to *flip and turn* their states of mind. Use *your* positive attitude and enthusiasm to create environments conducive for success. You can do this by homing in on one key resource—your people power. You can be a catalyst to help other people feel more hopeful and positive when challenges seem to be overwhelming them.

Remember, *everyone* has challenging days. And the people you're communicating with are no different. Assist them in hurdling over obstacles, and help them make their days better.

I have done some of my best work when a client was having a difficult day. For example, early in my career I would sometimes receive a call from one of my largest clients—typically late on a Friday afternoon. That person would be quite upset. His or her computer network was down, and several hours had passed since someone from my company had been called to fix the terminal.

Since the client was unhappy, I would go over to his or her office and make calls to our customer service department until a technician arrived. Sometimes, it would take several more hours for someone to show up. So I would stay there until 8 p.m. or later. While I would rather have gone home at 5 p.m., the few extra hours I spent in those clients' offices made all the difference in their attitudes.

I took those Friday night lemons and used them to make lemonade attitudes. My presence and assistance helped the clients' attitudes turn from sour to sweet. They are prime examples of flip and turn.

Sure, on those stressful Friday evenings, I could have looked at my watch and stood up at 5 p.m. I could have announced that I was going home, and hoped that a technician would soon arrive. However, I wake up every day determined to make a difference. I assist those who need my help and give them a kind word or a vote of confidence. With this attitude, you cannot help but win more friends and influence more people. Going beyond the call of duty makes the biggest difference.

Take your eyes off yourself and concentrate on helping others with their difficulties. This not only benefits them but also helps you put your own challenges into perspective. Giving of yourself is part of using your people power, and it separates you from those who don't. You will also have opportunities to recognize and respond to the needs of others, which don't always directly relate to what you are offering. Care about others by assisting them with their challenges, no matter what they may be. It's key to being a friend and building high-touch relationships.

Have a caring, attentive attitude toward others, and understand that everyone enjoys a nice conversation and a bit of fun. This is essential for you to succeed with people. When done correctly, with other people's needs at heart, this communicates your sincerity and charm. There is nothing more delightful, all the way around, than being honestly concerned about and assisting others. The important part is to focus outside of your own needs and concentrate on those of others. Use your ability to flip and turn their attitudes from negative to positive. Then continue to be resourceful and kindhearted as you support them in getting what they want and need. You'll find that in taking care of others, you'll feel good about yourself—and you'll actually be taking better care of yourself as well!

Mirror, Mirror on the Wall...

We generally communicate from one of two different perspectives—we think either about ourselves or others.

When people think about themselves, they are focusing on their own wants and needs—not those of other people. When we communicate with others, it's natural to want to talk about ourselves. However, no one wants to hear you brag or complain about your problems.

I remember many times being on a joint sales call with a new or struggling salesperson. It irked me when he or she sat in front of a prospect and focused only on how great our company and its service was compared to the competition. Now don't get me wrong, self-confidence is certainly an asset; however, self-praise is a killer. I would later explain to the salesperson that he or she might as well have been speaking to a mirror. The entire conversation was self-centered, rather than focused on the other person.

I would then continue by telling the salesperson to start thinking about others. When you direct your attention toward them, your breathing relaxes. Show others you care by focusing on them, thereby creating an atmosphere where ideas can be freely shared. You'll better understand their points of view, and be totally present and participating, as they share their wants, needs, and feelings. Do this while maintaining a natural balance of giving and receiving. It shows you care about them. As a result, they will most likely care about you in return.

At the next sales call with the now-enlightened salesperson, I'd pull out a mirror and ask him or her to look into it. Then I'd say, "Turn the mirror around." As long as the mirror was turned around, I explained, it was time to let the other person speak.

When we walked into the next prospect's office, the salesperson and I had our imaginary mirrors facing the other person. This reminded us to listen. We learned about the prospect's objectives, gained a better understanding of his or her wants and needs, and won the sale. We focused on the prospect, not ourselves.

Always think about other people. Relate to them with a positive attitude and show you honestly care. This will help create the win-win situations that allow them to sincerely connect with you. The best way to make good first impressions is to first let other people make good impressions on *you*. Help them bring out the best in themselves by focusing on them. Ask questions and sincerely compliment them, as appropriate.

When showing others you care, always maintain proper boundaries. Don't be in their face or too laid back. Just be sensitive to other people's wants and needs. Maintain excellent eye contact and breathe slowly and easily, letting go of any tension you may have.

When I see a high-touch relationship builder in a social environment, I notice three things:

- A friendly, sincere smile☺.
- A natural conversation—not one that is forced. He or she is focused on the other person. His or her eyes are not wandering all over the place, in an effort not to miss out on anything else that may be going on.
- A fun-loving person who enjoys getting to know someone new. He or she does so with the hope that it will lead to some good things for both parties.

I also find high-touch relationship builders in terrific marriages, as in the following real-life examples:

- I see a caring husband and wife holding hands. One is opening a door for the other. They listen to one another while maintaining eye contact.
- I notice the little loving gestures: a hug, a kiss, or a bunch of flowers—for no particular reason.
- I hear the simple "I love you" that their children pick up on, too, even if they seem not to notice. (Kids don't miss much!)

My wife, Gail, and I always take time, even after over 25 years of marriage, to show interest in each other and what we're each thinking, feeling, doing, and saying. We consistently go out of our way to be *nice, kind,* and *good* to each other. Why? Because it builds confidence, shows we care, fuels our marriage, and helps us feel good about each other as well as ourselves.

When you help others by showing you care—with kind words or deeds, handshakes, or pats on the back—you will surely make new friends and gain new clients and associates. Many people are communicating mostly over the

Internet, which can be quite impersonal. So those who regularly, sincerely connect with others on a personal level will gain the most rewards.

The high-touch of interpersonal relationships is, and always will be, essential for success. Technology, as great as it is, can't care about or create the bonds with others that are necessary for success. Those are *your* personal responsibilities.

The Power of Gratitude Helps You Focus on Others

Every great relationship builder understands the power of gratitude. It is the key that unlocks the people power within you to be sincere, loyal, and giving. Once again, forget your own wants and needs and focus on those of others. Persistently focus on other people—so you can learn how best to serve them. The following example shows what happened when a salesperson lost his focus on the client.

It was 10:30 a.m. and six of us walked into the client's conference room. We set up and got ready to present. I opened with a corporate overview, and then handed it off to my line manager. Once he was done, he gave it over to his account manager who then did most of the presentation. We spoke for two hours, including a question and answer session. At the end of the presentation, we invited our client and his boss to lunch at a nearby restaurant.

We sat down in the restaurant after two hours of presenting, only to have the salesperson become aggressive and overbearing. He started to sell, sell, sell, and push, push, push—all of which turned off the client. He didn't even give the client a chance to order his food! All he was concerned about was getting the sale—rather than how he could help the client solve his problem. He would have been more effective had he been other-centered and cared about the client.

Here's what came out of his aggressive approach:

- The client was uncomfortable.

- The client was not relaxed.
- The client couldn't wait to leave.
- The client never got a chance to enjoy his meal.
- The client will never have lunch with that salesperson again, or give him any business!

A high-touch relationship builder would have focused on the client and done the following:

- Allowed the client to relax and share whatever was on his mind.
- Allowed the client to order his food.
- Allowed the client to eat.
- Over coffee or tea, summarized the conversation with appreciation and the steps needed to follow up.

The people you are meeting with will often bring up business first. So rest assured you will have the opportunity to focus on their wants and needs. But don't try to impress them with what you know. Simply express what you need to learn from them so you can be of service. This shows you care and helps you form relationships from which gratitude will flow.

High-Touch Relationship Building 101—*The Story*

I have spent my entire career earning the reputation of being a master high-touch relationship builder, and I truly love every moment of being one. I always go out of my way to be *nice, kind,* and *good* to others, no matter who I'm with or where I am. When people ask me why I do this, I usually respond with the following story.

I am a member of a private club in New York City where I love to take my favorite clients. On certain nights the club opens its doors to the public. This means that for a cover charge, you can get in if the doorman approves.

One summer night, I was standing in front of the club by the curb waiting for a car to pick me up and take me home.

While there, I started a conversation with a driver named Mike. He, for whatever reason, was unsuccessful in getting his passenger, Mr. Bell, into the club. I asked Mike if I could knock on the window and introduce myself. He said that would be fine.

I walked across the street to the black limo and tapped on the window. The tinted glass came down revealing a well-dressed executive. I introduced myself and gave him two of my business cards. I then explained that I was a member of the club and was willing to help him get in.

He quickly thanked me, smiled, and got out of the limo. I then walked back across the street with my new friend, Mr. Bell. We joined up with Mike, who, in addition to being his driver, was also his assistant.

All three of us entered the crowded hallway toward the main room. I introduced Mr. Bell and his assistant to the club owner, and we all socialized for awhile. Realizing that nearly an hour had passed, I said good night for the second time. Mike then walked me out so he could thank me.

Mike and I stood at the exit and shook hands as he told me, over and over again, how grateful he was. He then asked, "Why did you go out of your way and go through all this trouble for people you don't know?" I paused, smiled, and replied, "But now I know you, don't I?" "You have a point," he said.

The next morning I received a phone call. Mary, my assistant, came into my office to tell me a gentleman named Mike was calling. I picked up the phone, and sure enough, it was my new friend. He quickly got to the reason for his call.

"Mr. Bell wanted me to call you and personally thank you for what you did for him last night," Mike said. "He also asked if you would like to be his guest for lunch at *his* private club next Friday."

I looked in my appointment book and saw I was free. So I said, "Sure."

Mike also told me it was fine to bring a guest, so I did. However, he didn't tell me I would be having lunch with the CEO and president of one of the largest financial firms on Wall Street!

As you might imagine, the lunch was great. We had a lot of laughs and terrific food. We didn't discuss business much, other than his interest in what I did. This surprised me, based on who he was. After about 15 minutes of explaining my business, I stopped talking about it to pick up on a more casual conversation.

We spent about three hours together during lunch that day, and it turned out to be one of the most enjoyable luncheons I have ever had. We ended with an exchange of thanks and went on our separate ways.

A few days later, Mike called again and asked me to put a presentation together. "Mr. Bell would like to give you some business," Mike said. "He enjoyed your conversation at lunch, so gather up your people and come on in."

I put together a team, a presentation was made, and we got an order. Today, I do a great deal of business with Mr. Bell—a man I call a friend, not just a client. Now this certainly doesn't happen every day. However, if it happens even once in your life, you are still ahead of the game. Gratitude from a person like that could lead you to many more contacts and relationships!

No one committed to success takes a vacation from the work of building relationships. You virtually always need to be doing so, one way or another—hopefully positively and effectively. Successful people are continually meeting the next new person who may have the contacts they would like to know. They are always looking for the next order, a new associate, or something else, so they can meet or exceed their goals and round out their month.

When I go through a store and shop, or anywhere else, for that matter, I always stop and talk with everyone I possibly can. It takes time and effort, but it's worth it. Who knows who you might meet next? It could be someone who would be excited about what you're doing. Therefore, it's wise to talk to *everyone*. It costs you nothing to smile☺, say hello, be kind, and take an interest in others. It's fun to do, and it conveys an attitude that can get you gratitude.

They Forgot to Teach High-Touch Relationship Building in Business School

Business schools teach many valuable lessons about profits and losses, business plans, and financial analysis. As a result of my education, I always look at the net—net retained revenue versus gross profit—whenever I evaluate a new business strategy.

I always ask for a business plan when one of my managers bursts into my office with a grand new idea. I always meet with my salespeople if they are not meeting their goals. I am also keenly aware of each client's potential to give me more business the next time I walk through his or her door. Therefore, I am very careful about how I treat each of these people at every interaction—for both short-term and long-term possibilities. Furthermore, it's just the right thing to do.

I am competitive, gently assertive, and very achievement oriented—but *never* aggressive. I have been told that those first three traits are the keys to success. "Never let them see you sweat," is a familiar old saying. After all, sweating is often considered a sign of weakness. In today's business climate, there's no room for weakness—only strength and determination. I figure someone else is always waiting right outside my door to help my clients, and take their business away from me! So I am resourceful and pay attention to my clients. I am concerned about them as people—their wants, needs, and feelings. If I'm not, my competition may take them away from me.

Thank you, business school; I am most grateful. Since you didn't teach me how to build high-touch relationships, I was aggressive with people at the beginning of my career. This sure made things difficult for me, but it turned out to be a great benefit. The relationship challenges I experienced early on caused me to focus more on others. I had to become proficient on my own in caring about others and building high-touch relationships.

High-Touch-Relationship-Building Lessons They Didn't Teach Me in Business School

Business school taught me how to compete, read spreadsheets, and understand profit and loss statements. However, it didn't teach me how to be *nice, kind,* and *good*, nor gentle in dealing with the human condition. That was unfortunate. Without an attitude of kindness and respect, successful business relationships were difficult, if not impossible, for me to form.

Fortunately, you don't have to make the same mistakes with people that I did. You can make your relationship-building ability shine more brightly than you may have ever imagined. Apply these three lessons: the power to feel; the power to care; and the power to understand.

One—*The Power to Feel.* Do your best to show empathy for the emotional states and the circumstances of those with whom you are dealing. Take a moment to learn about their challenges and feel their pain or unhappiness.

My mother always told me, "When your belly is always full, you do not know what it feels like to be hungry." Her words have stayed with me throughout the years and have guided me all through life. Whenever I am communicating with others, I always consider their feelings first and approach them accordingly.

Two—*The Power to Care.* I care a great deal about my business. In fact, I do all I can to reach my goals each month.

However, I'm even more concerned about how others will feel if I am *not* kind, caring, and sensitive toward them.

Always care about others—put people first. Without caring relationships, you won't have much of a life. The quality of your relationships largely determines the quality of your life. Now this doesn't mean you don't take care of business; it simply means you need to do your business with care. That's the kind of attitude that can get you gratitude!

Three—*The Power to Understand.* Many people understand high technology and the meaning of a good business plan. However, to be effective in business, we all need to understand human nature. To help us do that, we need to know the answers to the following questions:

- What drives the people with whom I'm endeavoring to build relationships?
- Why would people buy from, do business with, or otherwise associate with me?
- Why would others work hard with me?
- Why would people value me in helping them?
- How can I make my relationships with others most productive?

Your answers to these questions will help you develop the power to understand, and more effectively communicate and work with others.

In summary, the very best thing you can do is to have a warmhearted attitude—*always be kind and do well for others.* This is the surest path to success and happiness. It can better enable you to receive the gratitude you desire, which you will have earned and deserve.

"If you want something and don't get it, that means you really didn't want it, or you tried to bargain over the price."

—Rudyard Kipling

—3—

Light Your Fire for Desire

"The way you develop your desire
does not automatically take care of itself—you need
to make it happen. The key is to keep your dreams alive and
hold your objectives before you."
—Tony Sciré—

The dictionary defines desire as—"1. a longing or craving for something that brings satisfaction or enjoyment. 2. an expressed wish; request." So how does desire affect your life? And how does it affect your ability to create change or build high-touch relationships?

Desire is the foundation, the spirit, and the reason behind everything we do. The *fire for desire* involves having passion for your work, and whatever else you may be doing or want to do. You cannot see or touch desire, nor can you pull it out of your briefcase like a prop or a sales tool. But you need it to build high-touch relationships.

Following your desire can be a way of life, and pursuing it can require sacrifice. Instead of surfing the Internet, doing maintenance activities, or socializing with friends, desire compels you to work harder, make one more phone call, or meet with one more person. Your desire needs to be strong enough to drive you to strive for your goals—again and again. Regardless of any previous setbacks, you keep going until you reach them.

As long as you go to bed at night with a sincere desire to reach your goals, tomorrow gives you another chance to do what you weren't able to do today. You are alive with opportunities as long as you light your fire for desire. It can continuously propel you to do whatever you need to do to succeed.

Just as a fire needs wood to keep burning, so does your desire. Keep communicating the "I-can-do-it" message to yourself, or your fire for desire will die and turn to smoke and ashes. Some people believe that you don't feed a wood-stove wood until it gives you heat. However, it doesn't work that way. First add the wood, then light the fire, and lo and behold, the heat will come!

The key is to keep your dreams alive and hold your objectives before you. Post them in words and pictures where you will see them regularly. For example, this will help drive you to talk to more people, whether you know them or not. Any fear you may have will melt away as you focus on what interests *them*, including *their* dreams, goals, and objectives. Most importantly, keep on going—never give up or lose hope. Keep stoking your fire for desire. Unfortunately, many people let their fires die and they quit on themselves. This is generally why they fail to reach their goals and go to the next level.

There are two distinct types of desire: *fad desire* and *obsessive desire*. Each has its own foundation and style. When you develop your fire for desire and use it correctly, it'll help you reach your goals.

As you learn about the two types of desire, pay attention to their styles. Determine which desire most fits you and how it has affected your performance. I tracked both types of desires for several years to determine which one top performers possess. My efforts paid off. I learned there are very distinct differences between the desires of low and high achievers.

Fad Desire Won't Help You Get Where You Want to Go

Fad desire is like cotton candy—sugar, water, and air. There's no substance to it. It's shallow and fleeting. I sometimes refer to it as window-shopping.

A good example of fad desire is when people see an infomercial and suddenly decide to get into shape. They buy expensive running suits and sneakers, and join health clubs. They're fired up.

They get up earlier, work out consistently for the first two or three weeks, and feel really pumped and excited. They can picture perfectly what their new, fit bodies will look like and how healthy they will feel. However, by the fifth or sixth week, losing a little focus, they decide to sleep in and miss a day or two of working out. They're still motivated, but they decide that missing a few days couldn't possibly hurt.

After three months, these people visit their gyms only once a week. They say that working out is still important, but other tasks always seem to need more attention. After four months, they don't bother to work out anymore. Their fire for desire turned to smoke and ashes—they simply lost their passion and quit.

Another example is what happens in business at the beginning of every month. Many salespeople and business owners are initially excited and eager to make their sales quotas or organizational expansion goals for the month. They call clients, prospects, and associates and meet with them every day for the first week. Then, during the second week, they slow down to perhaps three days of such activities. By the end of the month, they've slacked off so much that they don't bother to contact anyone at all. They are no longer burning with desire.

People with fad desire can cause any profession or organization to be perceived in a negative light. They are not sincere in caring about others, nor in building strong, mutually beneficial relationships. People will sense that and be less inclined to do business or work with them.

If you are not touching the hearts of others to sincerely help, and just relating on a factual level, they won't believe in you. You probably have only fad desire.

Due to the lack of creating true emotional connections, you won't be able to establish long-lasting relationships. Fad desire just isn't strong enough for you to do that. Fortunately, fad desire can be turned into obsessive desire. To help you do that, be kind and show your concern for others, while keeping in touch on an ongoing basis.

Obsessive Desire Is Essential for Success

For example, when someone feels obsessive desire and compassion and *senses a commitment* to help, he or she will realize the two of you have something that goes beyond just business. It is a genuine and special friendship on which he or she can depend.

People prefer to buy from, and do business, work, and associate with people who have become friends. When others feel you are genuinely concerned and realize you have the desire to help, they'll be more inclined to respond to you.

Your success depends on your ability to produce and maintain obsessive desire. If you are not obsessive about helping others feel special, then frankly, you have little chance of developing long-lasting, high-touch relationships. Furthermore, your competition may have obsessive desire and win those same people over.

Top performers are obsessed with achieving their goals. They have a strong passion to succeed. They feel their fire for desire in the centers of their hearts. Adrenaline flows when they think about the possibilities. They overcome whatever challenges they encounter. Their desire is with them every night when they go to bed, every morning when they awake, and throughout every day. It never fades. It only grows stronger with time. When you feel this kind of desire and continue to doggedly persist, *nothing* can stop you from reaching your goals.

Does this mean you'll fail if you're not obsessed? Not necessarily. It just means you have a greater chance of losing interest versus the top performers who *do* have obsessive desire. The difference between success and failure is usually determined by whether or not someone has obsessive desire. Winners never quit! They have obsessive desire.

Is obsessive desire a gift? It may be to a limited extent. But it can also be developed by those who focus on what they want. Nonbelievers, and those looking for a "free lunch," can develop obsessive desire only if they get rid of their "stinking thinking."

I have obsessive desire. I always wake up with the fire for desire to complete what I couldn't do yesterday. I—not a job, a boss, or anyone else—control my future! I go beyond expectations for everyone with whom I am working. I take the initiative by being there for them.

Whenever I spend a late night helping a client, my obsessive desire takes over. I do all I can to assist him or her in resolving the particular challenge, as well as nurturing our relationship. I know the next time he or she needs something I can provide, that person will become obsessive about giving me the order!

Developing your desire doesn't automatically take care of itself. *You need to make it happen.* You need to have a big enough objective—something you simply *have* to accomplish, no matter what—to propel yourself into action.

Those with obsessive desire need to be role models. They need to support the fad-desire people they're associated with, so they, too, can develop obsessive desire. It's the fire for obsessive desire that makes stars, creates leaders, and develops winners. Obsessive desire is deeply felt and is as solid as a rock. It's like a close friend who always sticks by you. It cheers you on, gives you hope, and encourages you to persevere, even if the odds seem to say you should quit.

Obsessive desire cannot be seen or touched, but you will know you have it—and so will those around you. While they might not understand your obsessive desire, they will most likely respect you for it. They may even want to help, buy from, and work or associate with you, because they are attracted by your enthusiasm. Some of them will avail themselves of whatever you may have to offer. Still others may become interested in what you're doing, learn from you, and eventually join you on your journey.

Without desire there is no spirit or hope. So always keep your fire for desire burning. You may not be able to convince everyone to believe in what you are offering or doing. That's okay. However, that's even more of a reason why *you* need to have obsessive desire. It's *your* responsibility to be the driving force behind your own success.

You can accomplish your desires only by building and maintaining win-win relationships. Stir the fire for desire in yourself into an obsession. Obsessive desire attracts others. Some will become infected by it and want to be around you, while others will develop it themselves. Obsessive desire drives all great relationships. You can't build high-touch relationships or succeed without it.

"*Top performers are obsessed with achieving their goals. They have a strong passion to succeed. They feel their fire for desire in the centers of their hearts. Adrenaline flows when they think about the possibilities. They overcome whatever challenges they encounter. Their desire is with them every night when they go to bed, every morning when they awake, and throughout every day. It never fades. It only grows stronger with time. When you feel this kind of desire and continue to doggedly persist, nothing can stop you from reaching your goals.*"

—Tony Sciré

"Your wealth is where your friends are."

—Plautus

—4—

Circulate to Percolate

*"No matter what job, business, profession, or community work
you may be involved in, circulating is key to your success."*
—Tony Sciré—

Do you have any idea why hamsters don't have any friends and never seem to get anywhere? Do you really care? Well, you might want to start!

If you know anything at all about hamsters, you know that they just love to run on the spinning-wheel-to-nowhere. They delight in going around and around, staying within the confines of their comfort zones. They never leave their familiar surroundings where they feel safe.

There are many people who act like hamsters! They play it safe by staying in their comfort zones. They spin their wheels day after day, night after night—doing basically maintenance or entertainment activities—stuck in their routines. They often sit at home in front of the TV or computer screen, looking for some excitement to relieve themselves of boredom. Then they wonder why they can't seem to meet new people and accomplish their objectives.

As a result, they often become depressed because they feel their lives are going nowhere. They may even try to eliminate the pain by overeating, drinking alcohol, or taking drugs. Could you be in such a repetitive cycle? In addition to getting help with any addictive tendencies, the way out lies in breaking free from the confines of your comfort zones. Those who don't circulate lose.

There Can Be Danger Lurking in Comfort Zones!

Our comfort zones are in our minds. They are our attitudes about certain ideas, situations, people, places, and things. For example, if you have been employed by the same company for several years, chances are you are in your comfort zone with coworkers and your position. You know pretty much what to expect. But that could change. What if there's a take-over of your company? Suddenly, other people are in charge. You may find yourself in danger of losing your position or getting laid off.

Say you have been living in the same town for a number of years. You know a lot of people, and you're familiar with the area. You have your daily routine intertwined with what the town has to offer. You're comfortable there. Then a big fire comes through and burns your neighborhood, and most of the town, to the ground. You're still in the same geographic location, but you're certainly not comfortable anymore. So you decide to move to a nearby town, where you proceed to create a new comfort zone.

Our comfort zones are familiar but not necessarily comfortable! We go or stay there when we don't want to "rock the boat" or create change. Maintaining the status quo may just be a habit. We may not even realize we're doing so, because we all operate in the familiarity of comfort zones.

Retreating to a comfort zone is an easy way to leave well enough alone. If we insist on staying there, however, many opportunities will pass us by. Change is inherent in every opportunity. If we resist change, things are likely, at best, to stay the same, or maybe even get worse.

I am often asked, "Is retreating to a comfort zone the same thing as burning out?" My answer is, "No!" Burnouts occur when people work too hard while failing to keep a reasonable pace. They often neglect their health, the people they care about, and other important things. Comfort zones can be created when people do things in a humdrum routine. They may be bored, but refuse to change simply because they are familiar with what they're doing. People can still burn out even though they may be adventuresome, on-the-edge types. They may frequently go out of their comfort zones outside of work, but that doesn't matter if they're bored at work. They escape from the grind temporarily, but that's all it is—a temporary escape. The dull routine that leads to burnout at work is still there.

Then there are those who have stopped growing, or never got started. They either retreat to or refuse to leave their comfort zones. They allow themselves to defocus, or they were never focused in the first place. They postpone doing the things that could take them to the next level in their work or personal lives. They engage in time-wasting, status-quo-perpetuating activities to avoid failure and rejection. It happens all the time. They always seem to be amazed that certain others are more successful than they are—and they attribute it all to luck!

You have probably seen people, time and time again, limiting themselves by staying in their comfort zones. Have you ever noticed this tendency in yourself? If so, be encouraged. We all need to make a concerted, sustained effort to be focused and on purpose in what we've set out to do. It's not necessarily easy, and it can be quite challenging. But if we succumb to the temptations of staying in our comfort zones, we won't make any progress.

Over the years, I have observed people who have worked too hard and those who didn't work hard enough—often in the same office. I have seen salespeople constantly on the phone calling new and old prospects, making appointments, visiting clients, and cold calling. They were in the relentless pursuit of the rewards that come only as a result of persistent follow-up. I have also observed salespeople who were constantly in the office chatting, complaining, doing nothing, and always wondering why things didn't work out or why their sales were so low.

Yes, working too hard can put anyone on the road to burnout. This is especially true if the person works most of their waking hours and consistently doesn't get enough rest. Almost anyone can do that in sports, business, or in any other arena for a limited timespan, especially while pushing for a special goal. But a long-term, steady diet of this schedule isn't recommended. Balancing and pacing are essential.

When I discuss comfort zones, I'm not referring to those who excel. I'm talking about average people—those who do *not* work hard every day and never do anything beyond average to contribute to their success. They *never* go out of their comfort zones—not even to pursue cherished dreams and goals! That's sad, and it's also a real showstopper for those who would like a promotion or want to expand their business or profession.

Get Out There and *Circulate to Percolate*

The *only* way you can grow in your business or profession, or in community work, is for you to *circulate to percolate.* This means consistently getting out there beyond the confines of your comfort zones.

As you expand your sphere of influence, you will become even more fired up about what you are doing. You'll start to percolate—like water boiling in a coffeemaker. That is why people sometimes say, "He (or she) is on fire." But feeling that way is not a trick of magic. It's just the nervous system reacting to positive self-talk. When you're on fire, more people will want to be around and work with you, leading to increased sales, associations, and agreements. You're enthusiastically getting out there, meeting new people, and building relationships. You're generating significant interest in what you are doing or have to offer.

Those who find comfort in complacency never circulate. That's unfortunate, because no matter what they may be doing, circulating is key to their growth. Success, especially in today's high-tech world, depends largely on the ability to meet, understand, care about, get along with, and help others. The high-touch approach to building relationships will bring you the best results.

If you're not out there meeting new people, exchanging business cards, and creating new contacts, you simply can't percolate! The reason so many people fail is *not* from a lack of knowledge. They fail due to a lack of taking action— they're not circulating. They're not excited. They're not starting or maintaining caring, win-win relationships.

The success you long for begins on the edges of your comfort zones. If you feel uncomfortable meeting new people, then celebrate! That is where your growth will occur. As you overcome that challenge, you give yourself a golden opportunity to accelerate your success. Take any discomfort you may feel as a signal that you're setting yourself up for growth. Grab a hold of it and run with it.

Make Excuses and You'll Limit Your Success

The average person makes excuses for not taking action. He or she may foolishly believe that the excuse is a valid reason when it's really only an excuse. Some people even describe an excuse as "a thin shell of truth stuffed with a lie." The excuse-maker is simply looking for justification not to do what needs to be done.

Some of the more common excuses include:

- "I don't feel like making any phone calls. All I'll get is voicemails and answering machines."
- "I'd rather play it safe. I don't want to appear too eager."
- "I don't want to take advantage of anyone."
- "I'm too stressed to go out."

- "Why bother? I'll never meet anyone anyway."
- "I hate those places. I'm not going anywhere."
- "I need to do some work in the office. I don't have time to go out to meet anyone."
- "I am just too tired to make any phone calls. The baby kept me awake all night."
- "I don't feel like going anywhere today. It's raining."
- "The competition has already cornered the market."
- "I don't know very much about the product."
- "I'm not good at meeting new people."
- "Why would anyone want to talk with me?"

Some people use excuses to protect themselves and justify staying in their comfort zones. The sad thing is they are sabotaging their own success. As we all know, no one can force anyone else to pursue his or her own objectives. It's simply a personal choice. Regrettably, some people prefer to stay within the confines of their own excuses, self-pity, and lack of motivation. Still others may give sales, business ownership, or community service a feeble try. But if they are not immediately successful at building new relationships, they quit.

It's up to you to choose to circulate and understand that the fruits of building relationships are available to you. It's also up to you to make conscious, positive choices and take decisive action, so you can achieve the results you want.

Many people are incongruent with what they say they want and what they actually do. They are unclear and weak in their intentions and never take the necessary action. Time and time again, they set themselves up for failure. Deep inside, we all want promising new relationships and the rewards of success. We may, however, be sending ourselves mixed signals by saying things like:

- "I really want to meet that person, but they look too sophisticated for me."

- "I keep missing my monthly goals. I know I need to meet more people, but I can't seem to find the time."
- "I keep trying, but I don't seem to be making any progress. I just don't know enough people."
- "I want to be successful, but I don't get the lucky breaks other people do."

If you keep doing the same old things, you'll keep getting the same old results! But when you circulate, you will percolate yourself out of any ruts you may be in. Unlike the mindless hamster, you have the power to jump off the spinning wheel, open the cage door, and run to achieve your new objectives. Each new day gives you a chance to create positive change. You have yet another opportunity to do what you need to do to create your new tomorrows.

Do you need to establish new ways of thinking about what you can and cannot do? Maybe you're telling yourself you are too old or it's too late to do something new. But don't you believe it! Take a lesson from Colonel Sanders, the founder of the American fast-food chain, Kentucky Fried Chicken. He was 65 when he started traveling throughout the southern United States with his fried chicken recipe. He presented it to every restaurant he saw, constantly getting rejected—over 1,000 times! But Sanders *never* gave up. He kept going until he finally got a yes.

So why did Colonel Sanders succeed? He circulated to percolate, never giving up. By his age, most people have retired. But Colonel Sanders didn't. He refused to stop! He chose not to dwell in his comfort zones. He removed himself from them by following a big dream. How about you? What is *your* big dream?

Create your own opportunities. Don't wait for new people to come your way. Go out and *find* them! Some people tend to stay with the same clients, friends, and associates, seldom searching for new ones. As a result, they stagnate. Always be out meeting new people, while continuing to nurture your existing relationships. If some of those people are negative, though, you may want to limit your time with them, as they can sap your precious energy. Seek to be around positive, supportive, forward-thinking individuals—people who are where and how you'd like to be. Associate with winners, follow their lead, and grow.

Most people prefer to go primarily where they are already known and accepted. They feel comfortable in familiar surroundings. The people are friendly, they know their names, and they don't feel out of place. They feel just fine fitting in with the crowd.

That may be nice, but ironically, those benefits also present the greatest challenges. Being in familiar surroundings is not always good for progress. How can you meet new people if you continually go to the same restaurants, professional clubs, social events, and other places frequented by the same people? Go out and visit new places and start relationships with new people.

It All Works Together

Consider the human body. Every organ and muscle needs blood and oxygen. If your blood doesn't circulate, nothing can function. This is similar to your thought processes. Without positive thoughts, your power and energy cannot function properly either.

When you exercise, eat nutritious foods, take appropriate vitamins, minerals, and other supplements, and otherwise take care of yourself, you can come alive. You'll have the energy you need to get going in the morning and keep going all day. With sufficient purposeful use of that valuable energy, you will become the person you want to be. This encourages you to expand your horizons even further, and to increase and upgrade your sphere of influence. Only then can you reach new heights.

I once heard someone say, "If you're not living on the edge, you're taking up too much space." But when you circulate to percolate you *are* living on the edge. Think about it. To have more success, you need to consistently go out and meet new people, befriend them, and help them get what they want and need.

Your contact list is one of your most valuable assets. It includes those who know you and how, and what you have done or can do to help them. How can you create or nurture friendships with these people and best serve them? Knowing this and doing so is key to achieving your objectives. It's fundamental, yet many people just don't connect well enough with others to get to the point where they can be of service.

So how can you open the door to be a friend to someone new? As vice president of a major international company, my responsibilities took me to many parts of the world. Some of the greatest contacts I have ever made simply started with a hello, a smile, and some kind words. Whether I was in New York City, Brussels, Rome, London, or somewhere else, it just didn't matter. People in every country always responded to friendliness and kindness in the same way.

Talk to People You May Have Ignored in the Past

You need to be talking with *all kinds* of people. Your comfort zones may consist only of talking to people who are similar to you. Stretch beyond those realms. That's the only way you can open new doors and get into places where you may have never imagined you could go. Again, broaden your horizons. Take a chance and risk meeting new people.

For example, one Friday, someone I had never met before picked me up at the airport after a ten-day trip to 12 countries. The last thing the average person would want to do is talk with the driver for an hour and a half. But by being a relentless high-touch relationship builder, I got into a great conversation with the driver, Bill. We talked about one of our mutual passions—music. He shared that he wanted to record a demo. I told him I not only had some information about that field, but contacts there as well. I gave him my home phone number and told him he could call me anytime.

One topic of conversation led to another, and I told Bill I was doing some public speaking. He then asked me where I was speaking. I replied with, "Wherever I could," since I didn't have an agent. Bill got really excited when I said that. He said that he drove for Peter Young, an agent in the entertainment industry. He asked me for a business card, so I gave him two. He promised to give one to Peter the next time he had him in the car.

Three weeks later, Peter called me. We met in town for a cup of coffee on a Saturday morning. The extra effort of getting to know Bill eventually led to much more than either of us could have ever imagined!

Here's another example of what consistently meeting new people can do. I was on a flight from London to Paris when I took advantage of the opportunity to talk with the executive vice president of a major telecommunications company. At that time, I had a friend in that industry who was out of work, so I spoke with this gentleman about him. As a result, less than two weeks later, my unemployed friend had an interview with my new friend!

You'll never know what you might be missing out on if you don't say hello, and take an interest in other people, when the opportunities present themselves. Even if you don't feel like doing so, *it always pays to be in the habit of making the extra effort.* This has been one of the key secrets of my success, and that of many others as well.

Always put in the extra effort and do what unsuccessful people refuse to do. Reach out with kindness and consideration for everyone with whom you come in contact. The relationships that could develop may prove to be very exciting.

Have you ever helped someone who was not already a friend? If you haven't, that's unfortunate. Aside from not experiencing the pleasure of helping a fellow human being, that person might have one day returned the favor. He or she could have given you a referral or helped you get an introduction to a key person or account. Or you may have learned about some valuable ideas that could have helped accelerate your success.

Be Helpful and Care About Others at Every Opportunity

One day a client called to inform me that he had lost his job due to a downsizing of his company. He was an extremely talented man and had held a very high position with a well-known firm in Europe. I had talked with him once or twice at different meetings, and we had developed a great rapport.

I didn't know him well enough to call him a good friend, yet I still offered to put his name out in the field. I told him I would stay alert for any opportunities that might be of interest. A few days later, I was in a meeting when another executive mentioned a position that was available within his company. I made a recommendation, and the talented man who had lost his job was offered this new position. As it turned out, he moved into a key role in buying and became an important contact for me!

Circulate to percolate, even though the payback may not be right in front of you. Your hello, smile☺, interest, and kindness will leave a positive mark on the human race. You have more influence than you may think.

Put Some "Romance" into Your Work and Other Activities

I often witness people stuck in what I call a one-dimensional rut. They visit with new people but never really get to know them. They fail to go beyond superficial courtesy to reach the next level in building their relationships.

For example, some people visit new business acquaintances simply because they feel they have to, not because they truly *want* to. This does not mean you need to adore the people you meet; however, look for the good in them and do your best to, at least, *like* them. The most successful people are always developing close relationships—within appropriate boundaries, of course.

Putting some "romance" into your work and other activities simply means—*loving what you do, caring about the people you are dealing with, and putting your heart and soul into it.* As you promote what you are doing, you need to love people, treat them with kindness and respect, and enjoy being around them regularly.

When I was in the field selling, I would get together with a client for a 7:30 a.m. breakfast meeting and then go to the office. Around mid-day, I'd leave for a lunch meeting with a new client, and later return to the office for a few hours. For those who could not meet with me for breakfast or lunch, I would meet them for dinner. It's important to be flexible, accommodating, and considerate of other people's schedules.

I was often jokingly accused of eating a lot. The highly professional, more serious clients would talk about me by saying, "He is always entertaining. When does he have time to sell?"

I sure didn't have a lot of money back then, but I succeeded anyway because I romanced my clients. While my competitors stayed in their offices all day, instead of getting out there and courting their clients, I employed a simple win-win strategy. I loved to feed my clients with passionate enthusiasm and concern about their wants and needs. They, in turn, loved to feed me with new orders! That's what I call success. Everybody's smiling and everybody's winning. The lack of money didn't keep me from romancing my clients. They enjoyed those precious moments, and I enjoyed creating them. It was tremendous fun.

As time went on and my success accelerated, I was able to take my clients to the best restaurants in New York City. I always got the best tables, the best service, and the best food—and I still do!

To build great relationships, you need to put some romance into what you're doing. You simply can't build relationships very effectively over the Internet, via your company's website, or your e-mail. When people ask me if my approach still works today, my response is simple: "People buy from, associate, and do business with live, breathing people—not computer monitors. People love to be served and treated well."

Here are some examples of various situations and venues you may want to consider using—to put some romance into your work and other activities:

Power Breakfasts—Many people do not want to or cannot be out of the office during the business day. They prefer to have short breakfast meetings before work. You could even meet just over coffee. It's a great, low-cost way to build relationships.

Lunch—Most people enjoy a break for lunch. Be creative and find new places close to where they work. Also, be efficient because they generally don't have much time. Once again, this can be a very economical experience.

Dinner at a Restaurant—People love having dinner. They don't need to be concerned about being out of their offices or work environments; therefore they can relax and more easily enjoy it. Whenever appropriate, have dinners instead of lunches. This will give you more time to bond with others.

If you are on a limited budget, it's perfectly fine to get together over a salad, a bowl of soup, a sandwich, a cup of coffee, a dessert, or even just a soda. It's an inexpensive and relaxing way to meet with people, and it offers you great opportunities to build relationships. It's the individual attention you give others that is most important—not the price of the food.

Dinner and a Show—This option is appropriate for the executive level. Clients will appreciate these kinds of venues when they want to develop really close business friendships. Be aware that this type of entertainment usually includes their spouses (perhaps yours too) and can therefore be expensive. Nevertheless, this is an especially great way for bonding, and it could be well worth the cost.

Sporting Events—Many people like sports, anywhere from high school to professional levels. The only drawback is that if it's a super event, your people may go, no matter what—*not* because they are interested in you or what you are doing. Be sure they enjoy being with you, and they're not just there for the event.

On a Golf Course—Many people love to golf, and it can be a great way to build business and other relationships. If you're into golf, do it whenever appropriate. You'll have your people's undivided attention for a few hours. It's not too costly and it gives you opportunities to build rapport in beautiful settings.

People Who Work Out at Lunch—People are doing more and more these days to stay healthy. Use this approach to join those who won't have a regular lunch with you because they prefer to work out during their lunch hours. Know their time frames and, if you can, schedule quick lunches after their workouts. I have one client who works out at noon every day. So, afterward, we meet for a light lunch at 1 p.m. Once again, be flexible and considerate of other people's schedules.

On a Boat—Few people can resist being on a boat. When you do this, include their family and yours, if at all possible. It is a great way to make friends.

If you are associated with others in what you are doing, several of you could charter a boat for a fishing trip or a dinner cruise. It's a terrific way to bond the group.

At Your Home—People who are in from out of town usually love home-cooked meals, which can be simple and inexpensive. Be sure to include their spouses or family members if they are traveling together. This is a fine way to bond with others and make everlasting friendships. I do this often, as it is one of the most effective ways of building relationships.

Self-Belief

Self-belief says that every time you wake up and begin a new day, you know you are going to make a difference. You believe you'll positively affect at least one other person's life, or a company's or organization's well-being. Self-belief helps you develop the ability to assist more people in solving their problems and achieving their objectives. It gives you the edge in sharing what you are doing or have to offer.

Self-belief conditions you to persevere through each day—meeting new people, building relationships, making presentations, following through, and keeping in touch. This is especially true when you may be ready to quit—on those days when nothing seems to be going right. You go forward in faith, knowing everything will work out for the best.

Self-belief is gained when you understand the impact you can have on other people—because of what you're doing. Every time you meet with someone new you can make a difference as a result of your friendship and what you are presenting.

What you do and how you do it can tremendously contribute to the success of others. For example, any product, service, or opportunity you may be offering needs to be of such quality that it meets or exceeds their expectations and requirements. Otherwise, the people you are dealing with may suffer. You need to have truly rock-solid integrity in your presentation and know, for sure, that you are delivering the very best. This further bolsters your self-belief.

Self-belief convinces you that you can circulate to percolate and succeed. It enables you to freely dream your dreams and persistently strive toward your goals to achieve them. As you repeatedly do this, your self-belief gets stronger, and you become more of an encouraging role model for others to follow.

Know You Can Do Admirable Things Too

One of my favorite activities is reading about accomplished entrepreneurs—especially those who have overcome serious challenges, particularly at the outset. I love to read about these achievers and I'm motivated by their rags-to-riches experiences. It helps me keep my own challenges in perspective and gives me great hope. And it can do the same for you too. Listening to these leaders share their stories and teachings on audiotapes or CDs is also very inspiring.

What interests me most about such entrepreneurs is that they are simply ordinary people doing extraordinary things. They envision the big picture while others fail to do so. Never giving up or giving in—they always persevere.

True entrepreneurs never allow themselves to be talked out of something they believe will work, even though others may have failed at it. They ignore the negative-thinking people who tell them they can't accomplish what they've set out to do—either because someone else tried it before and failed, or it's "unrealistic."

Another common thread I have found among entrepreneurs is that they all take risks. They *create* their own opportunities rather than just waiting for them to show up. All entrepreneurs have self-belief. When they run into roadblocks, they never look back and ask, "Why me?" Instead, they say, "Why not me?" and keep diligently moving forward—like the sun moving across the sky.

True entrepreneurs never focus on their failures. Instead, they may say, "That one got away, but I learned something from the experience." They pick up the pieces, learn from their mistakes, and keep moving forward. They know that as long as they keep doing what they need to do—like circulate to percolate—sooner or later, they will accomplish their goals.

Your Self-Belief—*Stop Trying and Start Doing!*

Once you have obsessive desire and qualify as singularly focused, you may need to develop a new self-belief. A positive self-belief kicks in when you take on the idea that you are a winner. You realize that others, just like you, have made *their* dreams come true, and *you* can too.

Each year brings new seasons in football, hockey, soccer, basketball, baseball, and other sports. A new season means new and renewed players with new beginnings and an opportunity to start all over again. As each team meets to practice, they dream of having a winning season. To increase the opportunity for the team to win, each player needs to believe that his or her individual contributions to each game can make a difference.

We all need to believe that what we contribute can truly make a difference—that we really matter in the overall scheme of things. Whenever we begin to apply ourselves and diligently work toward reaching our goals, we, too, in a sense, begin a new season.

Average players may say they are giving it their best, but their hearts really aren't in it. They don't believe great success is within their reach. If they fail to reach their goals, they might quit or simply smile and say they will "try" to do it the next time. That's the problem—they try. But trying doesn't make it happen. They need to actually *do* it! Try really means they don't believe strongly enough to do what they are saying. They don't have a deep sense of personal conviction that they can do whatever they set out to do.

Those with real entrepreneurial thinking will always be the superstars. Win or lose, they always outshine the average players. They strive to be their best and habitually go beyond the call of duty. They consistently achieve their goals because they strongly believe they can win. They don't try anything. They actually go out and do it. When you're thirsty, do you just try to drink a glass of water? No, you actually do it. So whenever you want to accomplish something, just go out and do it—and keep at it until you get it done!

Heartfelt empowerment, the kind that true entrepreneurs have, is the key to self-belief. It causes you to dig deep, stand behind your convictions, and do whatever it takes to achieve your goals. Self-belief whispers, "Keep doing what you know you need to be doing. Success will come." Self-belief instills the right mental attitude and the deep-down understanding that you have what it takes to win. You know you will reach your goals.

To be a top performer, start by believing you already are one. You will then begin doing what it takes, like circulate to percolate. It all starts with your belief in yourself and knowing that what you are doing is important. So stop trying and start doing! Begin meeting more people today, and you'll start percolating all the way to your next goal.

Creating New Self-Belief

You can build new self-belief as a result of understanding and using people power. Know your people-power resource components, take appropriate action with them, and build rapport with others. These are the three ingredients that fuel new self-belief. Couple them with your unwavering commitment to circulate so you will percolate. You and those with whom you are starting, building, and nurturing high-touch relationships will win.

To build or renew your self-belief, implement the following:

- Count your blessings every day—with gratitude.
- Be willing to stand above the crowd.

- Remember that you are unique and have something special to offer other people.
- Stop to say hello and take genuine interest in others.
- Take action and circulate to percolate every day at every opportunity. But don't just try it. Go out and actually *do* it!

Many people fear meeting others because they lack self-belief. As a result, they prefer to stay in their comfort zones, as tiresome as they might have become. When you circulate to percolate, however, you increase the belief that you can effectively communicate with others. You believe more strongly that you can make a difference when talking with them and presenting what you are doing.

"The ability to form friendships, to make people believe in and trust you is one of the few absolutely fundamental qualities of success. Selling, buying, negotiating are so much smoother and easier when the parties enjoy each other's confidence. People who can make friends quickly will find that they will glide instead of stumble through life."

—John J. McGuirk

—5—

Contacts Can Make You Contracts

"Keeping in touch is essential to building relationships
in business and in life, and the key to turning contacts into
contracts. Never give up on your contacts."
—Tony Sciré—

Use your people power as you continue to practice, develop, and refine your relationship-building skills. This will propel you toward rejuvenating your current relationships, while helping you cultivate new ones.

While you are in contact with these individuals and building rapport, you can develop positive, often unspoken, contracts between you and them. You are in tune with each other and understand that, at some point in time, you'll do business or work together. Mutual trust is developing. This creates the atmosphere for an inventive spark to be ignited inside you, helping you increase and sustain the fire for desire. It releases your energy, and helps you develop the obsessive desire you need to accomplish your goals. Get moving and invest your time and ambition in goal-achieving activities so you can continue turning contacts into contracts.

Keep in Touch with Your Contacts

As mentioned earlier, one of the most important assets is your list of *contacts.* It's something you'll always have, unless, of course, you forget about or ignore the people on it!

Never give up on them, and don't let them fall into the hands of your competitors.

Think about how hard you have worked and how much time you've invested in starting, developing, and enhancing your relationships. All too often, though, people give up on their contacts. They believe they don't need to keep in touch with those who said no.

Always stay in touch with your contacts. Even if they move to an area or take a position where they can't do business or associate with you, stay in touch. Remember, things are always changing in people's lives. New opportunities to work with and serve them are always possible.

For example, I know a great salesperson in New York City who had a case of burnout. We'll call him John. John felt as if he just couldn't sell anymore. So, one day, he decided to leave his position. He bought a small food store in his hometown and opened for business. What I remember most about this fine salesperson is that, once a month, he would call just to say hello. He'd say, "Hi Tony. I'm in the shop today and was thinking about you. I just called to say hello. Hope all is well."

Even more incredibly, John also did this with every one of his old clients. Now, I had nothing at stake in his business, nor could any of his old clients do a thing for him in the new business he chose. However, as a high-touch relationship builder, John simply liked to call everyone each month just to say hello and keep each relationship alive. Whenever he was in town, no matter what the reason, he would always call and ask me to have lunch, or just meet him for a cup of coffee.

Before my friend bought his food store, he was my biggest competitor. After he left the industry, the people with whom we both had good relationships would always tell me when they got their calls from him. They would regularly say, "I miss him in our industry," or "They don't make salespeople like John anymore." Whenever I was with a client who said that, I would look at him or her and think, "What am I, chopped liver?" (By the way, I don't recommend that you ask this of yourself!) Nevertheless, I appreciated why John's clients felt the way they did about him.

If I actually happened to be with one of my clients when John's call came in, I always made it a point to notice the look on his or her face. I observed how expressive each one became while talking with him. John's monthly phone calls told his clients they were special and worth remembering. How simple, yet powerful, is that?

"I'll Be Back!"

I distinctly remember the day when my friend left our industry to buy the food shop. In many ways I envied him. He was getting out of the "rat race" and "putting his bag away."

At John's goodbye dinner, he whispered into my ear, "Tony, I need a break. However, there is a good chance I may come back into the industry one day if the opportunity presents itself." I laughed and said, "You are out of this business and starting a new career. Enjoy it." We then both dropped the subject and had a terrific time that night.

Two years later, during his monthly call, my once-strongest competitor said he was back in my industry. He had found a position with a new company that he just couldn't refuse. So he sold his store and started selling again. You just never know what might happen next!

The Moral of the Story

When you are a true high-touch relationship builder, you never, ever, give up on your contacts. Stay in touch with them, like cherished friends or relatives. You could call simply to say, "Hello, how are you?" or "Hope all is well." Let them know you've been thinking about them and were just wondering how things were going. To close, you could say, "Make it a great day!" That's all staying in touch involves. Those short, friendly calls are more appreciated than long-winded, high-pressure calls to push something.

Most people disconnect from others way too often. They never call unless they need something, want something, or have something to sell. This is unfortunate, because *keeping in touch is essential to building high-touch relationships, and the key to turning contacts into contracts.*

I always teach people that the greatest assets they have are their contacts. Your Rolodex® file, or however you maintain your list of contacts, is your insurance policy for continuing success. I call it *the power of the Rolodex®*. Never give it up or let other people control it. If you don't have contacts, you'll limit your potential.

Knowledge Is Power—*Use It to Benefit Others!*

Before you can make contracts with your contacts, you need to be knowledgeable about whatever you are doing. This helps you to be more believable, respectable, and credible, and more people will come your way.

If you are new to an industry or activity, be honest about it. Write down any questions people have that you're unable to answer, and promise to get back to them. This gives you more opportunities to build relationships with them.

As you begin, you may also be able to rely on the credibility and knowledge of your boss or another leader who may be mentoring you. Ask him or her to come with you to observe and support you while you make your initial presentations. Introduce your prospects to this person and tell them he or she can answer any questions you can't. This builds your prospects' confidence in you and your company or organization, and can help turn them into yeses.

The very best people in any arena are those who build high-touch relationships, and share their knowledge with others as part of developing interest and rapport. They are convinced that what they are doing is of value, and they have a believable approach. They also have integrity and respect for others' boundaries, and create credibility with every word they speak.

Previously, we talked about putting some "romance" into your work and other activities. However, successful people *never* make that a substitute for being knowledgeable. A nice breakfast, a great lunch, a fine dinner, a popular show, or an exciting sporting event can all be pleasant experiences. But these activities won't help you if you aren't knowledgeable enough about what you are doing.

Your success relies heavily on other people's perceptions of you, and whether they believe you can be truly helpful. Build stronger bridges of trust by generously sharing your knowledge. It helps build belief in you and what you have to offer. This, of course, supposes you care about these people and are developing rapport with them. You're not just robotically reciting facts, figures, features, and benefits. It all works together.

Whenever I hear someone say, "Tony, I'm afraid to stand up and speak in front of all those people," I am confident they lack sufficient knowledge about what they are presenting. The more you get to know your subject, the better the chances are of overcoming any fear you may have of speaking to a group of people.

As your relationships continue, it will become increasingly necessary to provide more detailed information than you did at the outset—when you were just generating initial interest. Enthusiasm can carry you a long way with people, but they will eventually need solid direction and assistance. You'll need to become the expert guiding them! It's impossible to lead others until you are knowledgeable about what you are doing.

So, again, be sure to take full advantage of whatever information and education is available to you. It will shorten the learning curve for you as well as those you're helping.

Getting acquainted with people is one thing. However, you need to go beyond that. You need to have them respect you for who you are and what you know. Fortunately, you can acquire the necessary knowledge and experience as you go, and earn their respect along the way.

If you are just starting in an industry or activity, you won't be expected to initially know as much as an expert. Nobody starts anything as an expert. Make it a priority to gather more information, so you can learn more and be of greater service.

Start by being enthusiastic and become a consummate student of whatever you do. Learn everything you can about it. Then become knowledgeable about the people you are dealing with, as well as about their families and their hot buttons—their dreams, goals, and objectives. Mastering the two can help you accelerate your success.

So what's the best way to learn? Jump right in and give it all you've got! Become more knowledgeable and expand your contacts as you continue moving forward.

Increase Your Sphere of Influence by Using *The Power of 2* Business Card Technique

As mentioned in the Introduction, this is the technique that inspired the title of this book. Earlier, I shared some examples of how I've used it.

No relationship, agreement, association, sale, or business can be created until at least two people communicate. When it comes to growth and expansion, two is always better than one: two contacts instead of one; two sales instead of one; two new associates instead of one; two agreements instead of one; two contributors instead of one. And *exchanging two business cards with each person you meet is better than exchanging just one!*

When two people first meet, they normally exchange business cards. This may lead to some new business or association, but probably only between the two of them.

Regularly exchanging *two* cards, however, not only generates goodwill but can also create business *beyond* the two of them.

Granted, not everyone you meet may want or be able to take advantage of what you are offering. But by using *The Power of 2* business card technique, you are planting seeds for potential referrals. Each of those people may know *others* who could be interested in what you're doing, either now or later. This can turn your meeting new people into *double* win-win situations, as each referral could lead to still another, and so forth! (Remember the example of doubling a penny?)

Always exchange two business cards with everyone you meet. Tell him or her you'll keep one for your records, and give the other one to someone you know or meet who could use what he or she is offering. This person will probably be quite happy to take two of *your* cards as well—one to keep and one to give to someone else who could possibly benefit from meeting you! Exchanging two business cards could significantly increase your sphere of influence.

Use *The Power of 2* business card technique every day as part of your relationship-building activities. For example, I'll never forget the day when I walked into the executive office of the head of telecommunications at one of New York's largest banks. We had a 10:30 a.m. appointment to discuss a major opportunity with a group of high-level executives. We all entered the meeting room and the first thing we did was exchange business cards. I began by giving two of my cards to each executive. One of them said to me, "Why two cards? I only need one. Why waste another card on me?"

I replied, "It's never a waste to share cards with people you respect. If possible, I would also like two of *your* cards. I was over at Banker's Trust the other day and your name came up in a very positive conversation. I told someone that I was seeing you this week and promised to let him have one of your cards. He told me he was meaning to give you a call. I believe your card will remind him and make it easier for him to do that. So I would like to keep one card for my file and give one to my friend."

He responded, "Excellent. Thanks. That was very thoughtful of you to remember me like that."

I said, "Thank you. If you know or meet anyone who may be interested in speaking to me, please give them the second card."

He quickly said, "Without a doubt. I'll remember."

I developed this practice one night while networking in New York City. I was busy building relationships and passing out my cards, when I got into a conversation about a mutual client, Bill, with whom I had lost touch. I asked this person if he ever met with Bill anymore. I had been meaning to call Bill, but I had lost his phone number and hadn't met anyone who knew him—up until then.

The person I was talking with shared that he saw Bill all the time. So I gave him two of my business cards and asked if he would be so kind as to pass one on to Bill the next time he saw him. I then asked my new friend for two of his cards. I would keep one for my records, and pass one on to someone I knew or would meet who may need *his* products.

At that moment, I recognized the tremendous relationship-building value of exchanging two business cards. It didn't take long before I began to develop the reputation for having created *The Power of 2* business card technique.

Here's a sample dialogue you could use when you begin using this powerful tool:

"George (or Susan), it has been a pleasure meeting you. I would like to give you two of my business cards, one for you to keep and one to pass on to someone else you know or meet who may enjoy speaking with me. In turn, please give me two of your cards so I can keep one in my file and pass the second one on to someone who needs to meet you."

The potential results of habitually giving out two business cards are very exciting. But always be sure to ask for two cards in return to keep the process mutually beneficial. That way, the other person benefits as much as you do. It can help *both* of you increase your contacts, so no one feels used.

Give the extra cards *you* receive to others you know and meet who could benefit from meeting the people who shared two cards with you. This shows your respect for the people and what they are doing, since it honors the agreements you made to give away their extra cards. This can increase the spheres of influence of all parties involved—both directly and indirectly.

After you have given each person's extra card away, be sure to tell him or her you did so, and to whom. This lets that person know he or she is important to you and allows you to create the ultimate double win-win, as well as other follow-up opportunities. Who knows? The people you met who said no to what you are doing may appreciate your sharing their card with others so much that, at some point, they may want to meet with you. Your generosity in sharing their cards with others may have struck them so positively that they will want to take a serious look at what you might be able to do for them!

Focus on What You Want

Focus, according to the dictionary, is defined as—"to fix or settle on one thing; concentrate." To turn your contacts into contracts, you need to focus. All successful people know the power of staying focused. Unfortunately, I have seen far too many people who are disorganized, and as a result, they "self-destruct." They didn't see their dreams, goals, or objectives clearly, so they couldn't possibly focus on them.

Dedicate yourself to your goal or objective and sincerely desire to achieve it. Then focus on it.

To focus, you need to create a vision of your goal or objective, a strategy for accomplishing it, and a plan for following that strategy. I often hear people say, "I wish I was home today." Or when they're home, I hear them say, "I wish I was out working today. I'm bored." When they are at work they want to be at home, and when they are at home they want to be at work. They aren't focused and have little or no idea what they want or where they want to be in life. They aren't aiming for anything except, perhaps, surviving until Friday or their next payday or vacation.

Focusing also includes making clear decisions. Being focused helps you intelligently decide what to pursue. It could be a certain type of work or business, a particular hobby, fulfilling your true potential, a community activity, or going after anything else you want out of life.

When we look at people like Bill Gates, CEO of Microsoft, and the late Bill McGowen, former CEO of MCI, we find some striking similarities—especially in their abilities to focus. For example, Bill Gates always makes it a priority to keep improving the product that launched Microsoft. Year after year, he works on making Windows® the world's best software—*by staying focused on it*. His success comes from his ability to focus on his core competency, and not deviate into other industries. Likewise, Bill McGowen had a policy not to buy or get into other businesses that would detract from MCI's telecommunications business. He focused on enhancing his product line with a family of telecommunications services. As a result, Gates and McGowen both became very successful—by focusing on their core competencies.

Just as Bill Gates and Bill McGowen each focused on his core business, so you need to focus on your core relationships. The ability to develop other people's loyalties, and have them provide you with referrals and recommendations, is key to your continuing success.

Previously, we covered people power, action, and rapport—*people par,* if you will. As in golf, to play par with people, you need to focus on them. If you ever watch a champion playing professional golf, notice how long he or she focuses on that little white ball and the hole—before taking each shot.

Focus to create and implement an effective people-power process in your work and other life activities. Focus is key to the quality of your relationships, as well as to your success.

Goals can be reached only when you firmly focus and take action in these five key areas:

1. Contacting, courting, and building relationships with new people.
2. Setting appointments, making presentations, and closing deals.
3. Constantly making phone calls and keeping in touch.
4. Nurturing your current relationships.
5. Serving people whenever possible.

Having fire for desire is essential for releasing the energy and positive emotion needed to focus. And self-belief is key to developing the firm foundation that enables you to consistently focus and grow.

As you focus, you can create a path to strategically move in the best direction, while putting your people power into action. The rapport you establish is evidenced by your ability to focus on and create harmony in your relationships, through your honest and caring communications.

Many people undoubtedly laughed at Bill Gates, Bill McGowen, and also Steven Jobs, founder of Apple Computers, when each of these three giants got started. That's just inevitable whenever anyone does something different than everybody else. So if others doubt you, laugh at you and what you are doing, or otherwise put you down, it's time to tightly hang on to your dream, and run hard on faith. Solidly know where you're going, stay focused, and don't let yourself get rattled by anyone or anything. Critical people are often just envious, wishing they had the guts and gumption to pursue *their* heartfelt desires. Don't let negative comments discourage you in any way. No one else pays your bills, and there are no statues erected to critics! Go for what you want.

Always keep sight of what you want to accomplish, along with your purpose in life—your reason for living—which needs to include helping as many people as you can. The successful people you have just read about did not give in to discouragement, nor did they allow anyone to suppress their dreams.

Top performers never quit after failure—even though they are sometimes faced with seemingly insurmountable difficulties, such as, tragedies, illnesses, and losses. They wisely use those challenges as stepping stones to success—as tools to learn what *not* to do the next time. True achievers believe they can make a difference. They do it in music, medicine, business, science, engineering, high technology, charitable organizations, and in every other industry or arena as well.

Throughout the ages, champions have persevered, never giving up. They just kept going until they reached their objectives. They all had strong, focused visions, and never just passively waited for things to come their way. They *created* their own opportunities, picked their targets, and focused on hitting them. When people asked them to stop or told them they were crazy, they respected the nonbelievers' points of view, but were never dissuaded. They maintained a positive attitude, stayed on course, completed their objectives, and fulfilled their dreams. In the process, they helped a lot of other people.

There isn't a scale in the marketplace that can weigh your desire. Nor is there a court or a judge who can determine whether it is right or wrong. You are the scale and the judge. Only you can determine whether your objective is right for you and your family. Be a top performer. Pick your target and courageously focus on it, so you can clearly see where you are going. This will help you stay on track until you get there.

You Are on Your Way

You are now primed for greater success. Build your list of contacts, develop rapport with others, and turn those contacts into contracts. Stay in touch with people—even if you're not now doing business with them.

Learn your subject thoroughly so your believability, respectability, and credibility grow with your experience. If you are a novice, defer to your boss, leader or mentor, and other experts in your industry or arena. Ask them to support your credibility as you acquire the knowledge you need to be more effective. Also become knowledgeable about the people you are dealing with, including learning about their wants and needs, so you can better serve them.

Use *The Power of 2* business card technique to expand your sphere of influence, and teach others how to do it too. Always go for double win-win results. No one can ever have too many contacts!

Finally, do whatever it takes to get and stay focused on where you're going and what you need to be doing to get there. Implement your plan of action, moment by moment, hour by hour, day by day. As you go along, you'll find more and more of your contacts turning into contracts and friends, perhaps for life.

"*Simply give others a bit of yourself; a thoughtful act, a helpful idea, a word of appreciation, a lift over a rough spot, a sense of understanding, or a timely suggestion. You take something out of your mind, garnished in kindness out of your heart, and put it into the other person's mind and heart.*"

—Charles H. Burr

—6—

Create Verbal Magic

*"What you say, how you say it,
and the method you use to say it are
key ingredients in your success."*
—Tony Sciré—

To be truly successful, in whatever you do, you need to create verbal magic. It's the ability to communicate with enthusiasm and passion, while maintaining integrity, to effectively reach people. This gives you the greatest possibilities for building mutually beneficial, high-touch relationships.

Today, there are many ways to communicate with others. This can range from a one-on-one discussion to speaking in front of a large audience, to using high-tech tools like answering machines, voicemail, e-mail, faxes, and phones. But just speaking or sending words versus truly connecting with people are two entirely different things.

While technology provides us with wonderful communication devices, unless we connect with others and build high-touch relationships, our success will be limited. High-tech tools can offer only low-touch experiences. They simply cannot be used to reach people like verbal magic can. A lot of people, in the name of "efficiency," kid themselves into believing that communicating with high-tech tools can replace talking with people. What do you think about that?

As for me, I love talking to people—whether it's at a one-on-one meeting or to a large group. I never substitute using high-tech tools for the high-touch relationship-building capabilities of verbal communications. In fact, speaking to a room or convention hall full of people who are waiting to hear me is one of my greatest thrills. Yet, people always ask, "How can you get so excited about speaking to all those people out there? Aren't you scared?"

I reply, "Of course I'm scared. In fact, I'm frightened to death. My knees get weak. My stomach gets queasy. I'm always afraid I'll do something silly." But since I go ahead and speak anyway—in spite of that—so can you!

It's what I *do* with my fear that makes the difference. I use it to get excited because I know what I'm presenting can help others. I take my eyes off myself and focus on sharing with the audience—it's people power in action. You may be surprised at how this can help you get through your speaking challenges. You can do just about anything when you're excited enough and know you can help others. Enthusiasm and a giving heart are contagious.

My fear motivates me to be my best—to push the outside of the envelope of my abilities. Use any fear you may have to motivate yourself as well.

Part of the solution in overcoming the fear of speaking is using actual fear-relieving approaches in making presentations. This will be covered later. In the meantime, know that commitment, self-confidence, and determination are attitudinal factors that help in successfully combating fears.

When you're solidly committed, there's no turning back. You act regardless of your fears. You know it's up to you to do what you need to do—and you do it.

If your self-confidence is a bit shaky, bolster it by reflecting back on previous accomplishments. Recall the positive emotions you felt at that time. Say to yourself, "I did that then, so I can do this now."

Determination is central to all success, and it stems from commitment. It's unrelenting persistence. Regardless of how many times you need to do something to get the results you're after—just keep on going.

In addition to the above, you may also need to develop self-respect. *Respect yourself enough to follow your dreams and do whatever it takes to reach your goals and objectives.* That's powerful! Go back and read that again.

As mentioned earlier, your belief in yourself is essential as well. If you don't believe in yourself, at least some, why would anyone else? Even if you believe in yourself just a little, that's a great start. Continue pushing yourself to get out there talking to more people. Your self-belief will skyrocket.

Always be humble in everything you do, and ask for help whenever you need it. You may be an expert in another area, but maybe not yet in creating verbal magic and building relationships. So be patient with yourself in the process.

The Key Aspects of Any Presentation

Always be enthusiastic in delivering your presentation, while forming a solid foundation of knowledge about your subject as well as your audience. Then you will be on your way to effectively conveying to others what's in it for them.

There are two aspects to any presentation: the primary one is your platform or message, and the secondary one is your signature or style. Both are essential in creating verbal magic and building relationships. Each requires a lot of dedicated work to make your presentations successful.

The dictionary defines platform as—"a body of principles on which a person or group takes a stand in appealing to the public; a program." It's the heart of your talk, which is topic and information driven, consisting of substance and detail.

The definition of signature is—"any unique, distinguishing aspect, feature, or mark." This is where you let your personality shine and develop your presentation into a charismatic delivery. Your message comes alive and becomes something special that can truly reach the people and get them moving your way.

Putting the two aspects together will enable you to deliver a masterful presentation. Having thoroughly prepared, you are then ready to WOW your audience and let your knowledge, sincerity, enthusiasm, and credibility shine through.

As a help, you can look to role models for some ideas, which I will encourage later. For now, though, let's talk about developing a strong platform or message, and coupling it with your own signature or style.

Here's what you need to do:

First—*Create a Strong Message.* What do you want to communicate? Will what you are offering help others improve their work or personal lives? Could it be the solution to their problems, help them reach their goals and achieve their dreams, or perhaps help them grow?

Does your message have substance? Have you eliminated any hype? Can you back it all up with facts, figures, and true stories? Is it interesting?

Before you give another presentation, be sure to answer the following questions:

- What if you lost your notes five minutes before a presentation? Could you still face your audience with confidence, assuming you didn't lose any slides or other visual aids you may have had?
- Could you freewheel your topic if you were asked to speak impromptu?
- What is your objective? What do you want to get across in your message that gets their attention, creates impact, and calls them to action?
- What material will you need to successfully execute your presentation?
- Do you need to learn more about your topic? Do you know enough about it to accomplish your objective?

Consider your answers as you prepare to make your presentation as compelling as possible. This will help you determine if it meets your audience's needs. If not, you may want to ask more questions, or do more research, to get the appropriate information.

Be conscious of using extraneous words. Avoid repeating yourself and using fill-ins such as um, you know, uh, and ah. They can make you sound unsure of yourself and your subject, and you may come across as less knowledgeable. Also speak understandably and clearly, while articulating key points with confidence.

People often ask, "Why is style secondary?" The reason is very simple. You first need to have a strong, compelling message. Otherwise, your presentation will be shallow, and the audience may not be as respectful as you would like. The primary objective is to *be thoroughly knowledgeable of your topic.* Your style can certainly enhance your presentation, but people, first and foremost, want to hear your message—*they want to be informed.*

Second—*Develop Your Style.* Your style includes body language, which is how you carry yourself, your posture, eye contact, facial expressions, head, arm, hand, leg, and other body movements. For example, standing up straight communicates self-confidence. Your style also includes your tone of voice, verbal inflections, and pace. You need to be so honest in presenting that your body language automatically supports your vocal characteristics with strength and determination.

If possible, always maintain eye contact with various people in the audience. Mentally segment the audience and focus on someone in each segment, thus connecting with the people in it for a period of time. Then move on to the next segment. When you're in front of large audiences, however, the lights can be so bright that eye contact is virtually impossible. That's something you'll get used to as you go along. As some speakers do, you may want to ask that the house lights be turned on, at least briefly, so you can visually connect with the audience.

Be sure your facial expressions match what you are saying. If you're telling the audience you are excited, look like it or they won't believe you. And be sure to make your head movements congruent with your message. For example, when you present something that can really help the audience, smile and nod up and down as you share what it can do for them. If you shake your head no, how could they possibly believe you?

Always ask if a mike is available. If so, be sure to use it. If not, project your voice loudly enough so the people in the back of the room can clearly hear you. Just ask, "Can everyone hear me okay?" Speak in an authoritative, yet pleasant manner, and take command of the presentation, using your voice inflections to emphasize key points. Always do your best to hold your audience's full attention.

Talk with purpose and a mastery of your subject, so the audience gets the point of your message. If you're getting a lot of puzzled looks, you may want to pause and ask them something like, "Are you with me?" and, perhaps, interject a bit of humor.

Are you polished and professional? Do you carry yourself in such a confident manner that you command respect from your audience? Do you feel passionate about what you are doing? Do you have obsessive desire? Are you really excited about it? Do you exhibit charisma? Or are you just robotically pushing whatever it is you have to offer? Are you communicating your message with honest emotion and enthusiasm? Or are you bored and showing it?

How do you plan to persuasively get your message across to your audience? How can you best communicate your knowledge in a caring manner so that the audience will listen to you intently, and understand the benefits for them? For best results, always be sincere, passionate, and knowledgeable about what you are presenting.

Are you communicating clearly, dynamically, and convincingly and, thereby, creating verbal magic? If it's naturally dry material, how can you jazz it up? Could you have some fun with it? How can you get and keep the audience's attention? This is all part of your individual style or signature. Make it a positive one.

Your Message and Style Checklists

Before you make another presentation, evaluate your message and speaking style. Use the following checklists to make sure you're on the right track:

Your Message Checklist
- Do you present your message in a logical, organized fashion, point by point?
- Is the heart of your message persuasive and does it meet your audience's objectives?
- Does your message represent your points accurately and positively?
- Do you avoid repeating yourself and using fill-ins?
- Do you avoid insulting and alienating the audience, for example, by not sharing off-color, ethnic, or debasing jokes?
- Can you answer most any question that may arise, even if it is negative?

Your Style Checklist
- Do you use a mike? If one isn't available, do you project your voice so it can be clearly heard in the back of the room? Do you ask if everyone in the audience can hear you okay?
- Do you convey authority with your tone of voice? Does it help you take command in a pleasant manner?
- Do you modulate your voice to emphasize key points?

- Do you speak at an understandable pace—not boringly slow, yet not so fast that you lose the audience's attention?
- Do you know your topic well enough that you don't have to depend on notes?
- Do you maintain eye contact with various segments of the audience?
- Are your arm and hand movements meaningful, and do they add emphasis and passion to your style? Or do they distract and take away from it, causing you to lose the audience's attention? Is the audience spending more time following your hands than your message?
- Do you tend to move around randomly or fidget? Are your movements purposeful?

What About Your Appearance?

In addition to your message and style, your appearance is also an important factor in the audience's acceptance of you and your presentation. Your grooming and attire need to be appropriate to the audience and the venue.

Here is a checklist to assist you in making an excellent appearance:

Your Appearance Checklist
- Are you dressed appropriately for the audience? For example, if you are speaking to executives, dress like one. It makes a statement and shows you respect them as well as yourself.
- Is your hair trimmed, washed, and combed? Is your total hygiene within acceptable standards? Are you fresh, shaved, and deodorized? Is your perfume or cologne subtle rather than overpowering?
- Are your clothes and shoes neat and clean? Are you conservatively dressed? Take the time to look crisp and professional. Your credibility is partially dependent on it. People remember what they see, as well as what they

sense, hear, and feel. You want them to focus on your message, rather than something you're wearing. Women with flashy earrings, low-cut necklines, tight clothing, or short skirts, as well as earrings on men, can be quite distracting.

- Do you display an assertive and positive posture with confidence?

Position Yourself Before You Speak

Arrive early, look around the room, and get familiar with the surroundings. Then locate the spot where you'll be giving the presentation. Stand there and look for key areas in the room that would logically make up the segments of the audience. This little extra effort could help you feel more comfortable and confident when it's time to speak. As a result, you won't feel out of place when speaking. Instead, you'll feel at home—as if you belong there. You surveyed the room and made the appropriate choices. You have assumed ownership of the environment.

Depending on the venue, you may want to arrive early and greet everyone at the door, perhaps without identifying yourself as the speaker. Then, when the members of the audience see you speaking, they will be delighted that you had taken the time and were friendly enough to have greeted them. As a bonus, they are likely to feel more comfortable with you and be more receptive to your message.

Consider Your Audience

The people you speak to will all have different levels of knowledge. What do they know about you? How versed or competent are they in your subject? Are they starting from scratch or are they already somewhat knowledgeable about your topic? Know all of this so you can adjust your talk accordingly. It will help you connect and move your audience into taking the action you desire.

Don't assume every audience will listen to every word you say. Be ready for virtually anything, whenever you speak. Who knows what may happen? The electricity could go out. The audience could have just had a big meal and may need an animated presentation to keep their attention. Or any of a number of other things could happen.

Here are some more questions for you to consider before you build your presentation:

- Do you know the backgrounds of the people in the audience? Are they executives, managers, blue-collar workers, business owners, homemakers, volunteers, educators, government personnel, religious leaders, married couples, or people of varied backgrounds?
- Is your topic appropriate for your audience?
- Did you invest the time to ask some questions or do some research about the needs and wants of those to whom you are speaking?
- Can you answer, without hesitation, almost any question anyone could possibly ask? If not, are you humble enough to admit that and tell the questioner you'll need to get back to them?
- Have you decided when you'd like to take questions— as you go along or at the end? Have you integrated these instructions into your talk so the audience knows what to do?

Your answers to these questions need to be:

Yes, Yes, Yes, Yes, Yes, Yes!

Get and Stay Focused on Your Speaking Skills

When you believe in yourself and your abilities, and what you are doing, you are on your way to making more successful presentations. Always remember that your message is the heart of your talk, while your style determines its heartbeat!

Know your topic thoroughly, focus on it, and be enthusiastic about presenting it.

Focus on becoming a superb presenter. You may find you really enjoy it. You may realize it can help you make a bigger difference and choose to make it a greater part of your work or other activities. This can take a natural course because the more of a leader you become, the more opportunities you will have to give presentations.

When I evaluate speakers, I first determine the substance of their talks by the depth of their messages. I then look at their styles. I have always found that the best speakers know what they're talking about and speak with enthusiasm. They also know the results they want and focus on getting them.

The best speakers are also always prepared for virtually any situation. They know the importance of being flexible and creative as they encounter challenging people or circumstances. For example, if someone in the audience has a negative attitude and walks out of the room, an excellent speaker remains focused on his or her message and the rest of the audience. Perhaps the person who left had a rough day and was stressed out, or simply wasn't open to the message. That's okay. Don't take it personally. Things change. Who knows? That individual may be receptive at a later date.

Those who come across as polished, charismatic, knowledgeable speakers put their hearts and souls into delivering their messages. They offer tremendous substance in striking, impactful ways, causing audiences to take action.

How to Overcome the Fear of Public Speaking

Many people say they are afraid to speak to a large audience, or even to a group of only two or three. That's unfortunate, because ultimate success in business and in life requires presenting to people. Become proficient at sharing your knowledge and ideas, along with whatever else you may be doing or have to offer.

I recently read a survey of the top ten fears in life. Do you know what came in first? The fear of speaking to a group of people. Do you know what came in second? The fear of death. Can you believe that? Many people actually fear speaking to others more than they fear their own deaths. How about you?

Fortunately, you can overcome any public speaking fear you may have. It can often be done in just three basic steps:

> **First—*Practice.*** Nearly everyone who gives presentations gets scared. It's completely natural. However, the more often people speak, the better they get at doing it—making it easier to overcome the fear. Practice, practice, practice. Take every opportunity possible to speak to groups of people, and get their feedback whenever you can.
>
> Self-coach by practicing your presentation in front of a mirror. This gives you a chance to evaluate your movements and posture. It also allows you to watch your style and practice your eye contact. Even create an imaginary audience and focus on their faces.
>
> You can also practice presenting to your cat or dog! They won't laugh at you, I promise. Hopefully, they won't hiss or growl at you either, but anything is possible. Keep practicing until your comfort level comes up. Don't just stand there and read your notes out loud. Learn the subject matter so well that you eventually get to the point where you won't need notes, or use them only occasionally. And be sure to put some enthusiasm and personality into your delivery!
>
> **Second—*Create an Imaginary Coach.*** In addition to pretending you are in front of an audience, create an imaginary coach as well. Ask someone who has a style you admire—perhaps your boss or a favorite mentor or

leader—what he or she does to prepare for a presentation. Then, as you practice, pretend that person is your imaginary coach and do exactly what you think he or she would recommend.

Another self-coaching approach is to slowly count to ten and say, "I believe in myself." Look in the mirror and tell yourself that you are capable of doing a great job by delivering a superb presentation.

Think about the best speakers you have ever listened to, and self-coach by modeling what they do. As you gain more confidence by emulating others, your own personal style will develop. Your charisma will start to shine through, and more people will come your way.

Third—*Get into Speaking Shape.* Before every presentation, get into speaking shape. Get excited and expect to give the audience your best. Create high energy by projecting an optimistic, upbeat attitude. This will give you the confidence you need to do a fine job.

Would you agree that the audience doesn't want to see you fail? Doesn't it make sense that people want you to give a great presentation, so they can gain the information they came to hear?

Have you ever heard a speaker who was not doing well? What was your reaction? Were you empathetic? Did you root for that person and hope he or she could get on track and make the presentation a success? You probably did, didn't you?

The power of positive human relations is found in communicating well with others, and it can be one of life's greatest joys. When you speak, you are doing so to connect with your audience, not only intellectually but emotionally as well. The more verbal magic you create, the stronger your connection will be. The more effectively you get your message across, the more of a catalyst you are likely to be for the audience to take the action you desire. This is an important part of building relationships and making a difference.

Present Like a Champion

To create verbal magic when you speak, whether it's to one individual or a roomful of people, have something exciting, as well as informative, to say. Be passionate about your mission and whatever you are presenting. This is essential for accomplishing your goals and expanding your sphere of influence.

Would you get stirred up about your subject matter if someone else was presenting it to you? What level of clarity and conviction do you have? Do you have the obsessive desire needed to create enough verbal magic to drive the important points home, and get people moving in your direction?

Now let's go back in time for a moment, or two, and look at the power of two people whose obsessive desires created verbal magic.

Pretend it's the '70s. You are sitting at home one day and receive a phone call from an old friend, Steve. You chat about various topics before he picks up the pace of the conversation, and gets to the reason for his call.

"Do you remember how we used to dream?" Steve asks, in an excited tone of voice. "Well, I'm living my dreams now. I have been working on a special project. I haven't told anyone else about it—you'll be the first. I called you because I would like to give you the chance to join me on the ground floor of an exciting opportunity. I believe we have the chance to be a part of something new and big."

Steve begins telling you about his project—building personal computers in his garage. "I know this may sound crazy," Steve continues, "but about three months ago, I finished testing a prototype personal computer. I believe that there will be one in every home by the year 2000!"

Steve is firmly convinced that his home-built personal computer will sell. He has an obsessive desire and is totally focused. During the conversation, you learn that Steve plans to create an untapped market for his computer, believing that it will, one day, become the apple of everyone's eye.

Steve finishes sharing and then asks you a couple of point-blank questions: "Do you want to join me? I know it's a risk—it may even be a long shot—but there's room for both of us. Can I count you in?"

Remember, it's the '70s. At this stage in history, no one had ever heard of a personal computer. If you had been offered this opportunity, what would you have done? Would you have joined Steve Jobs? Would you have done it, not knowing Apple Computer would be as successful as it is today? Would you have taken the risk, made the move, and believed you could have made a difference? Would his verbal magic have convinced you?

Now let's continue on our journey into the past. It's still the '70s. This time, your good friend, Bill, calls full of enthusiasm. He tells you he has just started a telecommunications company to serve truckers who are traveling between St. Louis and Chicago. Bill believes his new company, MCI, can grow and become one of the leading telephone service providers in the country.

"I believe I can change history," Bill says excitedly. "I'm planning to compete with AT&T by offering people better service at a lower rate. When I do, telecommunications will never be the same. I will indeed make a difference."

If Bill McGowen would have shared this with you, how would you have responded? Would his venture have sounded exciting enough for you to have asked how you could be a part of it? Or would you have told Bill he was crazy and that his idea would never work? After all, AT&T is a huge company and no one had ever competed with *them* before.

Would you have joined Steve or Bill in either of their quests to make a difference? If you said yes, congratulations! You're in the open-minded, success-oriented minority. Most people laughed at Steve Jobs and Bill McGowan when they got started. However, they created enough verbal magic to attract all the investors, employees, associates, customers, and everyone else they needed to build the success for which their companies are well-known. Create verbal magic and present like a champion.

Commit Yourself to a Great Dream or Objective

Steve Jobs committed himself to Apple Computer, and Bill McGowan committed himself to MCI Telecommunications. Envision your success and commit to something grand. Then you, too, can go as far as you can imagine, perhaps beyond. Remember, success is achieved by ordinary people doing extraordinary things.

Commit yourself to a life built on pursuing an exciting dream or objective. Make it big enough to excite you more than anything else you could possibly consider. This is the foundational element which enables you to create verbal magic. People may laugh at you and say you're crazy. But guess what? You'll be in good company. So consider it a privilege. It simply doesn't matter what anyone else may think, say, or do. Just follow your heart.

If you haven't already found it, your obsessive desire will help you find and develop the opportunity you need to realize a great dream or objective. Once you find it, commit yourself 100 percent to being successful at it. It needs to be something you believe in that can help others, while it lights your fire for desire.

Focus so you can clearly see what you want. Then develop a plan to implement a dynamic, comprehensive, invigorating strategy to achieve it. This sets you up to make the wisest choices each day, which will help propel you toward your target. Use and fine-tune the skills you already have, while developing new skills, especially your verbal magic.

You are not really committed to success unless you take the necessary risk and do the required work. If you don't, you'll just be fooling yourself. Your actions reflect your genuine intent.

Are Your E-Mail Messages Blocking Your Verbal Magic?

E-mail is an amazing high-tech tool for sending messages. It's certainly quick and it can be efficient. But it is extremely low-touch in its ability to help you connect with others.

We are all working in the computer age where e-mail has practically become our spokesperson or, as I like to call it, talk-ware. And even though Americans alone sent over 610 billion e-mails last year, there is simply no way they could have been used to create verbal magic.

You may be shocked at how isolated and lonely many people feel. This ranges from children tucked away in their rooms reaching out through Internet chat rooms, to adults e-mailing others working in the same building. The human touch they crave is missing, and the desire for emotional connection and caring remains largely unfulfilled.

It is very easy to miscommunicate and harm, or even destroy, relationships if e-mail isn't used appropriately. This can happen especially if you are in a hurry, sending a negative message, or aren't particularly proficient at written communications. Written messages can be subject to considerable interpretation, because there's no personal interaction.

Never try to use e-mail as a replacement for a phone call or a visit when there's a need for a high-touch communication—especially in a new relationship or a fragile situation. The computer is just a tool. It can't be used to create verbal magic. People need to hear your voice and sense your concern, or see your eyes and feel the warmth of your handshake, or hug, if appropriate.

We all have the best of intentions when we go to write an e-mail to explain how we really feel about a miscommunication we've recently had. We don't have to face a possibly unpleasant one-on-one encounter at that point in time. The whole thing is over in a few paragraphs. No one can interact and give us positive or negative reactions as we're doing it. The communication is one-sided. However, we need to ask ourselves some questions: Did we *really* get our point across? Did the other person *feel* our sincerity and emotion? Did he or she *understand* our good intentions, or did the situation become even worse?

I would ask myself those questions *every* time I sent an e-mail in an attempt to resolve a situation. And I'd always get the same answers. I would never fail to lament that it would have been better *if only* I had just called those people to talk about the issues. Instead of investing the time to speak from my heart, I had let my nimble fingers do the communicating. The trouble is neither our fingers, nor does the computer, have any emotions. This makes it incredibly easy to send people unkind or even cruel e-mails.

So guess what? I changed my approach to heart first—fingers later. Instead of sending an e-mail that may fail to communicate my understanding and good intent to someone who is already upset, I make a phone call. For example, I may open with a simple, "Hi John, how are you? Hope you are doing well. I owe you a conversation. I know we may not agree. However, let's talk about it. Is this a good time?" So when you, too, have situations to resolve, always make phone calls and use your verbal magic to create heartfelt connections.

You might be surprised at the positive reactions you get in response to your sensitivity for others. They may either just listen or tell you how they feel about their situations. If they start talking, let them share—*without interruption*—so they can get all of it off their minds and hearts. They are more likely to openly communicate when you sincerely show your concern, and kindly share your thoughts and feelings. For example, you may even want to say something like, "I may be wrong in my thinking or in what I said. If so, I apologize. I just want to do the right thing—whatever that is. My desire is for us to have a mutually beneficial relationship."

Apologize for any way in which you may have been offensive or contributed to any misunderstanding. This could lead the other person to share what he or she thought was confusing or offensive, giving you more insight into the situation. After all that, you can work out any remaining issues or differences that may exist. The great benefit in overcoming such a challenge is that it can take your relationship to a whole new level. You can actually bond better with that person after you have successfully worked through a problem together.

Sometimes it can be useful to write out what you want to say before you make a phone call. It will help you think the matter through and gain clarity about the situation. Then make the call and have a caring conversation. If you are unable to resolve the situation over the phone, it could be beneficial to get together in person. It may sound old-fashioned, but it's essential for fine-tuning your communications and enhancing your relationships. It's truly the way of a high-touch relationship builder. You could follow up *after* the call by sending a positive, sincere e-mail, perhaps writing something like, "I truly appreciate your patience with me." But whatever you do, be sure to *call first!* Make the call and create a heartfelt connection with that person through your verbal magic. And teach others to do the same.

How Do Voicemails and Answering Machines Affect Your Ability to Communicate Your Verbal Magic?

Voicemails and answering machines are also tremendous high-tech tools that can help businesses and organizations run more efficiently. However, they can be inadvertently used to create roadblocks to building relationships, and thereby actually hurt business. Unfortunately, as you may have noticed, some people use them to avoid talking with others.

Have you ever made a phone call only to find yourself stuck in the quagmire of voicemail "jail," or just talking to an answering machine? How did you feel about that? Were you eventually able to reach that person and, if so, in a timely manner? Or did you find yourself calling, time and time again, leaving message after message, but never connecting? If so, ask yourself, "Is that individual really trying to avoid me or is something else going on?" Have you, perhaps, offended him or her in any way for which you may need to apologize? You could ask if you have offended this person and apologize in the next message you leave—just as we discussed in the e-mail example.

The natural reaction to someone not responding to the message you left is a feeling of being rejected. But don't take it personally. He or she just might be in a meeting, out sick, in the field, out of town, or on vacation. Or that individual may be so busy, perhaps under the pressure of multiple deadlines, that returning the call is just not important enough to him or her. Unfortunately, you are not at the top of his or her agenda!

The lack of a reply can sometimes be attributed to the fact that the person you are endeavoring to reach no longer works in that office or for that company. The voicemail box simply wasn't disconnected, nor was the greeting adjusted to reflect the change.

Admittedly, it can be frustrating to reach people these days—everybody is so busy. So to communicate your verbal magic, you need to be creative and persistent. For example, one thing you can do is to press "0" while you are listening to the voicemail menu. Perhaps you will get someone on the phone who can help you learn the whereabouts of the person you want to reach. He or she may be able to tell you the best time to call that person, or perhaps actually track him or her down for you. If you are unable to get an operator, keep entering other mailboxes until you reach someone who actually picks up the phone.

If the previous suggestions don't work, you could send a positive fax, e-mail, letter, or package—then follow up with another call. Some people respond more readily to these other forms of communication. If you send a letter, you could also include a sample, a catalog or brochure, a pen with your company's or organization's name on it, or a self-recorded audio-tape or CD with your message on it. You may even choose to send a little gift like a box of chocolates, a floral arrangement, an inspiring or uplifting poster, a book, or even a small teddy bear. Send something out of the ordinary to get his or her attention! A week or so after you've sent the letter or package, be sure to follow up with a phone call to ask if it has been received. Then maybe you can get a dialogue started.

A small, inexpensive gift can help break down any barrier that may exist between you and the other person. It can also brighten the day of someone with whom you already have harmonious, consistent interactions. However, regardless of anything, this, of course, needs to be done with utmost sincerity and good intent—not as a manipulative ploy. You know you can bring value to this person, and they can bring value to you. If none of these ideas work, then endeavor to reach someone else who works with or for that person, or perhaps a higher-up who might listen to you. Keep persisting until you connect. Then create verbal magic with someone who can assist you.

As you persevere to connect, have hope. The apparently indifferent person might leave the company. The replacement would be starting fresh and may well be very responsive to you. The two of you may be quite compatible, and able to communicate and build a strong relationship.

Now, let's look at voicemails and answering machines from the perspective of others striving to reach us. Are we doing the same thing to them with *our* lack of responsiveness? Are we frustrating them, like others may be frustrating us?

If you need to say no or not now to some of the people who are leaving messages, or refer them to someone else, are you doing so? Or are you letting them waste *their* time by leaving message after message? Are you showing you care enough about others to adjust your voicemail or answering machine greetings to reflect when you'll be in and out? Or are you giving them a contact person's name and number, if appropriate, so they can get the help they need when you're not available?

When people call and leave messages, either to ask for or give you help, do you consider those calls only as interruptions that don't warrant your attention? If so, you may need to look at the bigger picture. Ask yourself why you're in business, or how you can best serve your employer or organization. You may be preventing some great mutually beneficial relationships from ever getting started. This lack of responsiveness could also erode the relationships you already have. It could hurt your work, business, or something else in which you are engaged.

Remember, you need to respond to and do things for others to achieve the success you desire. Success isn't built on convenience. Look at interruptions as opportunities to create verbal magic and better serve others.

High-tech communication tools are wonderful when used appropriately. They can save time and help move business and other projects along. However, when they are regularly used to avoid talking to people, who are either asking for help or endeavoring to offer it, progress can be thwarted.

Verbal magic is key to developing high-touch relationships. Create it and you will enjoy more and better connections with others. It will lead you to greater success and happiness as well.

"While technology provides us with wonderful communication devices, unless we connect with others and build high-touch relationships, our success will be limited. High-tech tools can offer only low-touch experiences. They simply cannot be used to reach people like verbal magic can."

—Tony Sciré

"**E**ach of us makes his own weather—determines the color of the skies—in the emotional universe which he inhabits."

—Fulton J. Sheen

—7—

Master Your Emotions

*"People like to be around positive,
even-tempered, friendly, helpful people they like,
trust, and can call friends."*
—Tony Sciré—

A key component of relationship building is the ability to master our emotions. Fortunately, we can all control our emotions through the thoughts we think, the attitudes we carry, the choices we make, and the actions we take. We can let go of, or better control, any tendencies we may have to automatically react negatively to life, its challenges, and the people around us. Our emotions cannot control us unless we let them.

The happiest of us have learned not to let our own or other people's unskillful behavior, or the malfunctioning or break-down of things, get us down—at least not for long. We look for the good in everyone and everything. And what you look for in life is generally what you find. Your thinking and the attitudes you choose lay the foundation for your experiences. As Eddie Rickenbacker said, "I believe that if you think about disaster, you will get it. Brood about death and you hasten your demise. Think positively and masterfully with confidence and faith, and life becomes more secure, more fraught with action, and richer in achievement and experience."

Every day you make choices. They lead to the actions you take and the results you get. And how you respond to life each day as it unfolds is also your choice. You are responsible for what you do, how you approach doing it, and how well you do it. You are also responsible for your emotions. How do you react or respond to everything that happens and everyone involved? How do you treat yourself and others? While you don't have control over other people's emotions, you can *influence* them in a positive way by having an upbeat, friendly, helpful attitude.

When you come across a challenge in dealing with others, do you use it as an opportunity to strengthen your relationships? Or do you let your emotions get the better of you, to the point where you offend one or more people? Are you understanding and forgiving of others' inappropriate actions or reactions? Or do you lash out at them and make situations even worse? Maintain a positive attitude so you can master your emotions. This enables you to get the best possible results with others.

People make attitude choices every day, affecting their emotions positively or negatively. Here are some examples:

Positive	Negative
1a. I'm happy and upbeat, and having a great day. I look for the good in everything that happens. I won't allow anyone or anything to ruin *my* day.	**1b.** I'm sad, downbeat, and having a bad day. No matter what I do, nothing works. Everything's falling apart. So-and-so just ruined my day.
2a. I am smiling and it's contagious. I feel better when I smile, and so do others. The world seems a lot brighter to me.	**2b.** I don't feel like smiling. I'm miserable. Don't mess with me or I'll let you have it. The world is a terrible place.
3a. I'm laughing because I made another silly mistake. I'm just learning. I'll fix it and move on!	**3b.** I'm crying. I can't seem to get anything right—no matter what I do. I'm a mess, and I don't know what to do.

4a. I'm *nice, kind,* and *good* to everyone I know and meet, and I help people whenever I possibly can—because I care. I look for the good in others no matter how they may be acting at the time.

4b. I am manipulative, intimidating, aggressive, and ignorant. I don't trust anyone. I've gotten the short end of the stick all my life. It's a dog-eat-dog world. Besides which, nobody cares anymore!

5a. I say a cheerful hello to everyone I meet, no matter who they are. I realize that each one is a person of value, just like me, and deserves to be acknowledged.

5b. I don't bother saying anything to the people I meet. Most of them can't do me any good anyway. Furthermore, nobody gives a hoot about anyone else, so why should I?

6a. I love other people unconditionally, even if I don't like their behavior.

6b. I hate people—they're just pains in the butt and not worth bothering with.

7a. It's about time so-and-so and I had a talk. There's tension between us. We'll make peace and create a win-win situation—no matter what it takes to accomplish that.

7b. I'm in a bad mood and feel like ruining somebody else's day. I'm finally going to tell so-and-so a thing or two about how I *really* feel about him and his stupid project.

8a. I build great relationships and never work with strangers. I always build friendships with the people I meet, before I associate, or do business, or anything else with them.

8b. I just keep to myself. Why go to the trouble of meeting new people? They'll probably reject me. Who needs more new friends anyway? I already have enough.

Do you recognize your own attitudes in any of these examples? If you have a positive attitude every day, congratulations! But if you're just realizing how negative you may have been in the past, and how poorly you chose to deal with people and situations, be encouraged. It's easy to be negative. It requires practice to overcome years of negative thinking and the emotional reactions you may have had to life and its challenges. Like any new habit, though, a positive attitude can be cultivated, and will enable you to respond in a kind and caring way.

If you are feeling despondent, smile☺—even if you don't feel like it. You'll feel better! Then take positive action and help others. It's up to you to get moving, even if you don't feel like it. This upgrades your attitude which, in turn, positively affects your emotions. *What action will you take today to move yourself closer to your objectives?*

Jolt yourself out of lethargy by doing what you know you need to do. No one else can do it for you. Who will you call that you've been putting off calling? Will you go out, take an interest in others, make new friends, and share what you are doing as you go through the day? Will you brighten someone else's day with a sincere compliment?

Get excited and get moving! Do something toward your success and that of others. This will make it easier to master your emotions and be happy.

People are more likely to work, associate, or do business with you when you have a happy disposition. Happiness is a choice, and it's always *your* choice whether or not to be likeable. As the saying goes, "An ounce of honey will attract far more bees than a pound of vinegar." Be happy and most of the people around you will be happier too. You'll also develop better relationships.

The relationships you build, or fail to build, depend on the quality of your choices and actions. Take full advantage of your freedom to choose. Then take the action necessary to better your life. Achieve the mutually rewarding relationships, peace of mind, happiness, and prosperity for which you may be yearning.

The *Push Back* Approach Helps You Master Your Emotions

I learned this approach from a friend who observed my selling style, which in my younger days was forceful and overbearing. Back then, I was an impatient, emotional, in-your-face, aggressive kind of salesperson. I was anxious to succeed, and I believed the best way for me to do so was to push hard and sell, sell, sell. Boy, was I ever wrong!

My pushy and overbearing ways hurt me far more than they helped. I scared people. They felt it would take too much energy to cope with me. I've since learned that it is far better to push yourself back rather than be aggressive. Just be gently assertive. This approach enables you to develop better rapport with people and, as a result, be more successful.

Here are the basics of the *push back* approach:

- Always take an interest in other people's wants and needs, and ask how you can best serve them.
- Focus on and listen intently to their concerns, without interrupting them.
- Once they are done sharing, answer any questions they may have. Then ask them to tell you more about the things that interest them.
- Be calm so both of you can relax.
- Speak gently, with a pleasant tone of voice.

Perhaps you now realize that you may have been aggressive and emotional with certain people. That's probably why they haven't responded to your efforts to stay in touch. To help alleviate those situations, simply ask, "Have I offended you in any way? If so, I'm sorry." This can help you build bridges of care and concern, and repair any harm you may have done. As we discussed in the last chapter, you may feel rejected when that really isn't the case. Maybe those people were just stressed out and preoccupied with other demands. Give others the benefit of the doubt. Be flexible and forgiving—just like you want others to be with you. Be humble and ask the question, coupled with your apology—even if you don't believe you've done anything offensive. People will love it, and you will feel good about yourself for doing so.

Once Upon a Choosing Time

You have, no doubt, been in many situations where you needed to make a choice between various options. Each decision changed at least one area of your life, to one degree or another, and probably impacted your emotions as well.

So what did you do? How did you choose? Why did you choose one direction over another? What was the outcome? How did you feel about it? Were you pleased? Or were you disappointed? Would you do something differently if you had the opportunity to do it all over again?

You have the power to choose in most areas of your life. You choose your friends, your work, your outside activities, the things that are important to you, and where you live. You also have the power to choose how much you care about others and the way in which you treat them. But it's the attitude you choose that affects your emotional state throughout the day, and how well you relate with others.

Here are three choices you make at the beginning of each day that affect how you handle your emotions:

- You choose your attitude—to be positive or negative.
- You choose whether or not to care about yourself enough to pursue your objectives.
- You choose whether or not to care about others and take the actions necessary to help them solve their problems—so they can achieve *their* objectives.

Like you, no matter where I am, I begin every morning with me, myself, and I. When I get out of bed and look at myself in the mirror, I see my reflection. (Combing my hair helps with this!) I know that I can't truly care about others until I take an interest in myself and care about what I want, the way I feel, and the attitude I project. That has made all the difference in my success. *Ultimately, it was my choice to care about others that enabled me to succeed in life.*

Always strive to be your best. When you learn to be comfortable with and kind to yourself, you can then be comfortable with and kind to others. It all begins with a loving, caring attitude. Love others and they will, in all likelihood, love you back. It may sound corny. But it's true—and it works!

To succeed in your work or community and in life in general, wake up every day thankful for the gift of life. You've been given another chance to work toward accomplishing your objectives, while making a difference in other people's lives. This can't help but give you hope, and a new perspective of what you believe is possible.

True success comes from caring about others. But you can't give what you don't have. So you need to first care more about yourself and your objectives. This will reflect in the fine way you treat others, along with how you help them. It will show itself in your calm, friendly demeanor, and in how you support them with your attention, interest, and actions. When those you interact with know you care about and respect yourself as much as you care about and respect them, your relationships will grow to new levels.

I'm often asked, "Is it true that good-looking people have greater success?" I always respond by saying, "What is good-looking? Is it a person with a great face and body, or a person with a great heart and attitude?" People with positive, caring attitudes and emotional balance have inner beauty. This gives them a special glow, which most others cannot help but notice, admire, and love. I have seen some of the most physically beautiful and handsome people fail in relating with others because they depended too much on appearance. Looks can only go so far!

For example, conceited, self-centered businesspeople, no matter how physically attractive they may be, will not get very far in building relationships. Their success will be limited, because they're only concerned about what's in it for themselves. They fail to build bridges of care and concern. As a result, they often lose business to ordinary-looking but compassionate businesspeople, who reach out generously to others with their loving hearts.

The reality of life is *not* what you see on television or in the movies, where virtually everyone is a model or a famous person. In real life there are only real people, like you and me, who need and want to feel important and know that somebody cares about them.

Lots of ordinary people are doing not-so-ordinary things every day, and you can do likewise. For example, I see ordinary salespeople breaking new sales records, and forming lifelong relationships with their clients. But the only ones who accomplish those feats are those who believe in themselves. They project a positive attitude, acquire the necessary knowledge, and consistently reach out for and care about others.

Mastering emotions is a key element of success in any arena. I'm living proof of that. I'm one of those ordinary people doing not-so-ordinary things. I think positive thoughts, exhibit a positive attitude, control my emotions, and I'm gentle and caring toward others. I'm thankful for every day I'm given, and I always look forward to tomorrow. You need to do the same.

As long as you wake up tomorrow, you have another chance to do something for someone that you didn't do yesterday. What you did and how you were yesterday does not predict what you do and how you are today! You have choices. Today offers you a fresh new beginning to master your emotions, so you can better relate with others and achieve the success you desire.

"Jolt yourself out of lethargy by doing what you know you need to do. No one else can do it for you. Who will you call that you've been putting off calling? Will you go out, take an interest in others, make new friends, and share what you are doing as you go through the day? Will you brighten someone else's day with a sincere compliment? Get excited and get moving! Do something toward your success and that of others. This will make it easier to master your emotions and be happy."

—Tony Sciré

"What one thing does the world need most today—apart, that is, from the all-inclusive thing we call righteousness? Aren't you inclined to agree that what this old world needs is just the art of being kind? Every time I visit a factory or any other large business concern, I find myself trying to diagnose whether the atmosphere is one of kindliness or the reverse. And somehow, if there is palpably lacking that spirit of kindness, the owners...have fallen short of achieving 24-carat success no matter how imposing the financial balance sheet may be."

—B.C. Forbes

–8–

Continue Building the Relationship *After* the Sale, Association, or Agreement Has Been Made

"Following up, keeping in touch,
and showing you care—after the sale, association,
or agreement has been made—are essential
elements for long-term success."
—Tony Sciré—

Relationships grow and flourish only when you stay in touch with people and nurture them *after* the sale, association, or agreement has been made. Successful people realize that the closing of the deal, whatever that may entail, is *not* the end of the relationship. It's just the beginning!

For example, where was our salesperson on that sunny December morning? My wife, Gail, and I had just signed the contract papers and handed the title company a check for our new home in Florida. But once we had closed the deal, our salesperson never again responded to our needs.

It all started when Gail and I decided we would like to own a home in a warm climate. We spent six months shopping for our dream place, looking at all kinds of homes and villas. We finally found the perfect location on the West Coast of Florida. It had all the palm trees you could imagine, and numerous ponds that added to the area's scenic beauty.

This was the place we had been diligently searching for, and we wanted to build a house there. So we met with a salesperson who we thought really cared and wanted to work with us to help us make our dream come true.

Gail and I had put our faith and trust in the hands of this salesperson, who was the builder's representative. We had spent more than adequate time looking at models, checking locations, and deciding on the perfect house. We had been engaged in that process for six months before we finally went to contract. This meant the builder was committed to building our new home.

We left Florida feeling really good about our choice. When we returned home to Connecticut, we spent our time looking at pictures of the property, and showing our friends and family blueprints of the house. We also spent time planning the best way to decorate it to make our new house feel like a home.

The construction went smoothly for the first few months. And since this was the first house we were having built, we were quite excited about it. During the early stages of construction, our salesperson had sent us a picture of the house as it was being built. However, things soon changed from sweet to sour, and lo and behold, she quickly seemed to lose interest in us.

When Gail and I signed the building contract, we had set a target closing date of December 31st. This meant the builder could demand final payment on that date. We would have to settle, even if it required rushing construction or taking delivery of a home that looked as if it were still being built. We felt confident, though, that our salesperson wouldn't let that happen.

A month before the target date, the builder's office called to tell us we absolutely *had* to close by December 31st *or else*—even though the house wasn't finished. Gail did her best to reason with them. "It's Christmas season," she explained. "We live in Connecticut. Getting a flight on such short notice could be next to impossible."

Gail first endeavored to call our salesperson for some assistance, as soon as we learned that we *must* close by year's end. We thought she had our best interests at heart and would help us work through this challenge. Gail called again and again. Finally, after not getting a return call, and believing there was no other alternative, we agreed to close by December 31st.

Getting a flight, as Gail predicted, wasn't easy. We flew into Orlando, then drove three hours to get to the West Coast. Before we closed, we went to the house and there wasn't even carpeting going up the stairs!

Fortunately, a good lawyer, who truly cared about us, helped us close by putting money in escrow. We then moved on from that challenging situation.

To date, our salesperson has *never* called. She hasn't even come by our new home—which is directly across the street from the sales office. In fact, one day, when we were working outside, we watched her pass by without even waving or saying hello. Amazing!

Why am I telling you this story about our house? Our salesperson was literally nowhere to be found during the tough times. She was great only in the presale stage. *After* she had made the sale, she let us down. This is certainly an example of how *not* to treat others.

What Happens If a Relationship Is *Not* Nurtured After a Sale, Association, or Agreement Is Made?

One thing's for sure, our salesperson will *never* sell us *anything* again. Since the lots on each side of our home are vacant, we have considered building houses on either side for our children. If we ever choose to do that, we can guarantee you that our salesperson and builder won't get the sale. The salesperson's lack of interest in us, after we signed the contract, potentially lost $500,000 in new revenue for her company.

On top of that, we will *never* recommend that salesperson or builder to anyone else either. Whenever I am standing outside our house and a prospective buyer asks me about it or the builder, I feel compelled to tell them exactly what happened. When people ring the doorbell and ask to see the inside of our house, I gladly show them the poor workmanship. I also warn them that the salesperson will disappear once the contract is signed.

You are more likely to *lose* the people you're dealing with if you do these six things:

1. You lack sensitivity for them and their concerns.
2. You don't return their phone calls or respond to their other efforts to reach you when they have questions or concerns.
3. You are disinterested in helping them overcome their challenges, saying you don't have time.
4. You put them down even if your company is in the wrong. You make no effort to act on their behalf.
5. You prove they can't trust you by promising to do certain things, while failing to follow through or tell the truth. You never make any apologies.
6. You have a chance to do something nice for them but don't bother.

What Happens When a Relationship *Is* Nurtured After a Sale, Association, or Agreement Has Been Made?

I have never failed to make a sale, association, or agreement because I or my company ran into a challenge in meeting someone's request. I have found that failure occurs only when the presenter doesn't really care, and isn't sincerely interested in being helpful. For example, what if our real estate salesperson *had* returned Gail's call and said she would do all she could to help us? We would still be interested in working with her and giving her referrals. Even if she couldn't have helped, just returning Gail's call would have shown she cared. It would have made a world of difference to us.

Let's take a closer look at the specific ways you can build rapport *after* the sale, association, or agreement has been made. People are more likely to *stay with you* as long as you do these five simple things:

1. Keep in touch. Show them you are endeavoring to remedy any challenges they encounter. Be proactive and go beyond the call of duty, as you assist them.
2. Return their telephone calls, and respond to their e-mails, faxes, and other correspondence.
3. Empathize with them if your company is in the wrong. Do your best to help them, even if you're unable to change a thing.
4. Always do what you say you'll do and tell them the truth. Apologize and do everything you can to make up for any oversights.
5. Do nice things that prove you care and are sincere in your efforts to help them.

Lasting Success Is Built *Way Beyond* the Time When the Sale, Association, or Agreement Has Been Made

Many people disagree with me when I say, "It's easy to get the sale, association, or agreement." However, this is surprisingly true and has been proven again and again. Making the deal can be simple. The real challenge, though, may come *afterward.* Keeping people happy over time takes skill, patience, and compassion, and exemplifies the true meaning of building high-touch relationships.

Think back to when you made a large purchase—perhaps a new car. You probably spent a lot of money. After you signed the papers and drove your car off the lot, did you ever hear from your salesperson again? Probably not. How do you feel about that? Would you go out of your way to buy another car from that salesperson? I sure wouldn't.

Unfortunately, we are in a very transaction-based market of buying and selling. This makes it easy to get caught up in the day-to-day routine pace of cold calling and prospecting— forgetting about the base of people we've already established. Your prospect list is *not* your base. Your already-established client and associate list is your base. It consists of the people you have done or are doing business with, and also those with whom you are associating. Some people feel their job is done once they have a yes and have sewn up the deal. That's why *those who care enough to keep in touch long afterward stand out and will reap the most rewards.*

Keep in Touch with Your Base!

Earlier I mentioned the power of the Rolodex®. However, it's meaningless without people in it who remember you, and want to do business or continue to associate with you— because you stayed in touch. Always remember to protect and nurture your base.

The more enjoyable win-win relationships you create with your base, the more you'll be amazed at the wealth of information they'll share. That's why it's so important to keep in touch and build on your relationships *after* the deal has been made. People's wants and needs are always changing. *When you keep in touch, you learn what else you can do to further help your people.* You can also find out if they have any co-workers, friends, family members, business associates, or acquaintances who may be interested in what you are doing or offering.

Some people think that keeping in touch with someone in their base is a waste of time. They believe their time is better spent finding new prospects. My experience has shown it's best to do both. There is plenty of time. You can cold call new people and "old call" others you have closed recently or even a while ago. Keeping in touch has enabled me to learn as much as possible about what is happening with my people regarding what I sold them, as well as about any new concerns or needs that may have developed. In essence, I became their friend. If I hadn't stayed in touch with my base after the sales were made, I wouldn't be as successful as I am today.

Keeping in touch gives you the chance to halt many challenges before they begin. It also enables you to connect your people with individuals who could help them in other ways. Like me, you, too, can always have an endless supply of client and associate friends—people you can either do business or something else with in the future. Keeping in touch also makes it convenient for them to refer others to you. You're essentially developing a network of friends.

Over the years, I have heard some people say it is better to stay away from a client rather than keep in touch. Their reasoning is that if you see or talk to the client too often, you might be asked for a price reduction. This thinking is, without a doubt, mistaken. When you have good relationships with your clients, they aren't likely to ask you for a price reduction, unless your competition offers them a lower price first. However, if you've developed a truly great rapport with them, it will take a lot more than just a lower price to sway them away from you.

I have seen many salespeople lose accounts because they failed to keep in touch after they made the sale. As a result, their clients thought they didn't care. And they probably didn't, or else they would have kept in touch! I guarantee that you will continually lose relationships with others if you don't show them you care. Show you value them by keeping in touch.

Always remember to be appreciative of and nurture your relationships. This is key, especially *after* the sale, association, or agreement has been made. I practice this philosophy every day. I endeavor not to take anyone or anything for granted, and to be thankful in general. By far, it has been my greatest asset and sales skill. Make it yours too.

"*Three things in human life are important. The first is to be kind. The second is to be kind. And the third is to be kind.*"

—Henry James

—9—

Motivate Your *TONY*

*"No one else can meet new people or establish relationships
for you. You need to do that yourself."*
—Tony Sciré—

Every high-touch relationship builder has a
TONY—Talent Of Networking Yourself. Again, networking
is meeting new people and building win-win relationships so
both parties can accomplish their goals. People often ask
whether networking is *really* a talent. The answer is yes! It
is definitely a talent. And like every other talent or skill, it
can be developed through practice. Do whatever it takes to
tune up your *TONY.* It will help you build high-touch relationships and create the success you desire.

The Golden *TONY* Rule

Others aren't going to network for you, although they
may support you in doing so. How could anyone else possibly develop personal, caring relationships for you with other
people? To accomplish your objectives, you need to do your
own networking. It's as simple as that. *Get out there, meet
more new people, and build high-touch relationships.*

People who are building their businesses or careers are
always expanding their spheres of influence. No matter what
you're doing, you need to do the same for maximum success.

People may invite you out to meet others, but what you do when you get there is up to you. Your networking activities are your responsibility. Many people who need to expand their spheres of influence just wander around at professional gatherings and other networking venues. They talk either with no one or with those they already know. What good is that when they are in a prime venue to be networking with new people? This is just another example of people staying in their comfort zones. Later they'll say the gatherings weren't worthwhile. They didn't meet anyone new!

Creating your *TONY* is based on everything you say and do. It is very much like the 1980s movie *The Karate Kid.* Mr. Miagi, the karate teacher, had the student, Daniel, wax all of his cars in a very disciplined way. He meticulously taught the boy specific procedures that became habits. The young fellow was taught to apply the wax with a certain hand and arm motion. And when he removed the wax, he was taught to do so with another specific, effective motion.

While Daniel disliked waxing cars for hours on end, it helped him develop certain skills. Daniel disciplined himself by putting the wax on and taking it off with carefully synchronized hand and arm motions. This then enabled him to perform a move called the middle block. It helped him defend himself in competitions when someone would throw him a punch. The car waxing helped Daniel perfect his skills, which enhanced his abilities in karate.

This example shows how skills can be intertwined. You could benefit in other areas from the diligent practice of one particular skill, like networking, that may seem unrelated to anything else. However, it can help you reap future rewards in many unexpected ways.

Put Your *TONY* into Action

Now it's time to better develop your *Talent Of Networking Yourself.* Start by using your people power every time you see someone with whom you formerly had or currently have a relationship. Then begin developing your *TONY* at business meetings, conferences, social events, and wherever else you find people you haven't yet met. Remember, you can network anywhere there are people!

The first time you network you may feel uncomfortable or nervous, but that's okay. As you practice, it'll get easier and you'll become more proficient at it. Can you recall when you first learned to drive? You went from knowing little about it to becoming a licensed driver who is now comfortable on the road. It's the same way with networking.

A great time to put your *TONY* into action is during the hectic winter holiday season. There's generally shopping to do, parties, dinners, and other social events to attend. This is great. All of these activities offer more opportunities to network. Yes, the holiday season is a prime time to meet new people. Use them to gear up for the next year of sales, business expansion, or whatever else you are doing.

To get yourself out there and into meeting new people, attend as many holiday parties and events as you can. Work each room by mingling and talking with as many people as possible. I know some successful salespeople who manage to attend 15 parties in one week! They get together with people at breakfast, lunch, and dinner functions. This enables them to reacquaint themselves with those they may not see often during the year, as well as to meet new people. They may not write up any new orders right away. But by meeting and building relationships with new people, and revitalizing their current relationships, they're laying the groundwork for future business.

No matter what time of the year it is, it's always a great time to put your *TONY* into action. As an example, one year I met a salesperson who was so unique that I'll always remember him. In fact, years later, we still call each other simply to say hello and share how things are going.

What made this man so memorable was his passion for building relationships. He loved to be out meeting new people. He also enjoyed talking with, listening to, and nurturing relationships with those he had done business with in the past. He loved to reconnect with people who, for whatever reason, had not bought from him *yet*. If someone couldn't, or wouldn't, do business, he never let that bother him. He just kept a positive attitude, nurtured and maintained his relationships, and made himself available to serve people, if and when they needed him.

This salesperson was patient, and always waited until people honestly needed his products. Even if it took months for people to buy, he would still stop by or call once a week—just to say hi and learn about their current needs. The best part is his efforts always paid off. Those people remembered him. When they needed his products, they always called.

Create Your Own *TONY*

You may be asking how you can create or have a *TONY* of your own. Here are two suggestions to help you get started:

1. **Join Toastmasters**—It's a great organization that can help you get comfortable in front of a crowd. What I like most about it is that everyone's objectives are the same: meeting new people, making a few friends, learning how to feel comfortable speaking, and upgrading speaking skills.

2. **Work Every Room You Enter**—This means exactly what the five words say. It's something that requires work. In addition to whatever else you may be doing, always meet people and start new relationships. And remember to have fun doing it.

I know a fellow salesperson who goes on a mission whenever he networks. He never eats or drinks while working a room. He keeps his hands free for introducing himself to people and exchanging business cards.

He never wastes his networking time chatting with people he knows. His mission is to make as many *new* contacts as possible. If a friend comes over and tries to occupy his time, he politely says, "It's good to see you. But now it's time to circulate. How about giving me a call next week?" He then moves on because he's focused on his mission.

Without fail, he always meets new people and follows up with them on another day. He knows precisely when to proceed and when to back off. He's completely happy when he can shake people's hands, say a few pleasant words, and exchange business cards (two with each person, of course!). He saves his initial interest-generating discussion for when he follows up with phone calls to everyone. Then, at the end of each call, he schedules a time when they can both meet, so he can make his presentation.

Never attempt to close sales, or make associations or agreements, at social events. Use them as opportunities to meet new people, not close deals. But don't be shallow with your conversations either. Have meaningful discussions without spending a great deal of time with just one person. Pace yourself so you have time to meet as many people as possible. When you give each person your total attention, even for a brief period of time, you're more likely to be favorably remembered. Keep in mind that the people you're meeting may also wish to network with as many others as possible. They probably don't want to get bogged down in long conversations either.

I used these exact approaches when I developed my *TONY*. They've helped me meet *lots* of new people, many with whom I still do business. Be passionate about reaching your goals. Harness your energy and take action. With practice, motivating yourself and developing your personal *TONY* will soon become second nature to you.

"Just a little gift costing a dollar may give a thousand dollars worth of pleasure and be a lifelong grateful memory."

—John Wanamaker

–10–

Appreciate the People in Your Support Network

"Honor someone in your support network with lunch, a little gift, or a thank-you note."
—Tony Sciré—

In your quest for success be sure to remember the people who are helping you stay on track and reach your goals. Those in your support network, which may include people like your boss, coworkers, staff, employees, leader, mentor, friends, or family, deserve a great deal of gratitude from you.

I have yet to meet a successful person who doesn't have a strong support network. Having the right support can help you shine. It is one of the most important assets you can have to help you excel in whatever you are doing.

The People You Help Can Count on You, and You Can Count on Your Support Network

When was the last time you stopped to think about the kind of assistance your support network gives you? I don't know about you, but I sure owe a lot to the people who have cheered me up, cheered me on, and assisted me.

It can be very easy to get caught up in whatever you are doing, and forget about the people who stand beside and behind you, helping you day in and day out. They're often always there but, unfortunately, may be taken for granted. Chances are your support network has played a major role in the success you've achieved so far. They may even be one of the influencing reasons why you initially got into your particular business, field, or activity.

You undoubtedly know and care about the people in your support network. However, do you regularly show appreciation by thanking them for their assistance and consistently treating them with respect? Even if it has been awhile since they helped you, it's *never* too late to show them your gratitude. Surprise them! People love to be fondly remembered and appreciated—anytime! You'll feel happy and good about yourself for doing so.

Here are five great ways to show your appreciation:

1. A lunch.
2. An arrangement of flowers.
3. A box of candy.
4. A gift.
5. A thank-you card, note, or phone call.

Lunch Can Be a Great Time to Get Together

Think back to how many times you go out to lunch with others to specifically discuss business or whatever else you are doing. Even though these meetings are purposeful, isn't it also fun to get together in a relaxed atmosphere? Isn't it nice to have lunch and talk, as you nurture each relationship?

The people in your support network would also enjoy being invited to lunch. As soon as you can, call or see one of them and say, "You have given me a lot of help during the past few months, and I am very grateful. I would like to show my appreciation by taking you to lunch today or sometime soon. Your efforts have played, and continue to play, a major role in my success. And I'd like to thank you by having you join me for lunch."

Flowers Are Wonderful and Appreciated by Most Everyone

Flowers send a special kind of message that virtually everyone loves to receive. And when you give silk or dried arrangements, they can serve as long-time reminders of you and your thankfulness.

Did you ever buy flowers for someone in your support network to show your appreciation for his or her help? The next time you see a flower shop or floral display somewhere, pick up a small bunch of flowers and give them to someone who has assisted you. You'll love the look on that person's face as you present your gift. Take the time to show you care, and that you are truly grateful for the help he or she gave you.

Nearly Everyone Loves Candy

Candy—what a great invention! Whoever created it must have had two major objectives in mind:

1. It gives those with a sweet tooth something that tastes great and is fun to eat.
2. It also helps the recipients feel special.

Surprise someone in your support network with a gift of candy. It communicates appreciation. People ask me, "Isn't candy too romantic?" No way! It is a kind gesture and a great way to say, "You're playing a major role in my success. Thank you so much."

Giving a Gift Is a Wonderful Way to Say Thanks

How many gifts and little tokens of appreciation do you give to your support network? When you shower them with your gratitude by giving them small gifts, they're likely to love it. Big smiles are bound to come over their faces because it can be such fun to receive something, especially when it is unexpected. Watch the face of someone in your support network light up the next time you give him or her a little something. As a bonus, you'll feel good about having added a little happiness and joy to his or her life. When you give you also receive.

When I travel, I like to pick up a little souvenir, from wherever I have been, for the people in the office who support me. They are just small tokens of appreciation—nothing big or expensive—and another nice way to thank them.

Thank Yous Are Always Appreciated

Thank people in person, on the phone, or by sending them a card or note. If you really want to do something special, find out their birth dates and remember them with appropriate cards. This is a gesture they will always remember. Since very few people invest the time to stop and say thank you, you will stand out when you do. People always treasure appreciation, and you'll be glad you gave it.

Be sure to thank anyone in your support network who helped you accomplish something important. And, again, if you want to say thanks in a very special way, you can go a step further. Tell that person you are going to tell his or her boss, mentor, or leader what a great job he or she did in supporting you. Then do it. The next time you ask for support, your extraordinary expression of appreciation will be remembered. *You* were the one who put in the good word— *for him or her!*

The lunch, flowers, candy, gifts, cards, notes, calls, and other thank yous are all nice ways to give something back. You could soon become the most respected and talked about person in your circle. However, remember that all of those thoughtful gestures mean absolutely nothing unless you *truly care about those people* and *genuinely want to show them your gratitude.* If you're doing it just because you think you're supposed to, you won't enjoy it, and people will sense your lack of sincerity.

Make your thoughtful gestures really count by being truly grateful. Always do it because you value the people who supported you and played a part in your success. Show your gratitude whenever it's appropriate. And be sure to do it with love and heartfelt appreciation.

As the late Og Mandino, bestselling author, said, "...the deepest yearning of human nature is the craving to be appreciated." B.C. Forbes noted, "A word of appreciation often can accomplish what nothing else could accomplish." And Margaret Cousins observed, "Appreciation can make a day—even a life...."

If you've ever doubted the significance of being appreciative, hopefully that doubt is now gone! Show your appreciation to those who have helped you, and both you and they will feel good about each other. It's the way of a high-touch relationship builder.

"The way to make a true friend is to be one. Friendship implies loyalty, esteem, cordiality, empathy, affection, readiness to aid, to help, to stick by, to fight for, if need be. Radiate friendship and it will return sevenfold."

—B.C. Forbes

–11–

The Ten Commandments of
High-Touch Relationship Building

*"Practice successful high-touch
relationship building, and you'll enjoy the true
heart of your work and whatever else you do—the
people you need to care about and help."*
—Tony Sciré—

N ow it's time to ask yourself: "How can I consistently meet new people and build enjoyable, productive high-touch relationships, so I can reach my goals, accomplish my objectives, and realize my dreams?"

If you weren't quite sure before, I hope that you better understand high-touch relationship building and how you can most effectively interact with others. Practice successful high-touch relationship building, and you'll enjoy the true heart of your work and whatever else you do—*the people you need to care about and help.* The happiest people are those who have excellent relationships in all areas of their lives. They know that the best way to the top in business and in life is to build relationships that flower into friendships.

To help you stay on track, I have assembled what I call The Ten Commandments of *High-Touch* Relationship Building.

Live by them every day, and you'll have more friends, as well as a happier, more successful life.

Thou Shalt Be:

1. **Cheerful**—Wear a bright, sunny countenance at all times. Say hello, smile☺, and be *nice, kind,* and *good* to everyone you know and meet. Make friends and have fun everywhere you go.
2. **Healthy**—Think healthy thoughts and do healthy things. Exercise and maintain a proper diet, including vitamins and supplements, and eight to ten glasses of water a day. Use preventive measures like getting regular physical checkups, and get enough rest.
3. **Optimistic**—Create the positive power to accomplish your goals and make your dreams and objectives realities. Support others in doing the same. Look for the best in people and situations, and love what you do.
4. **Mannerly**—Help everyone you know and meet feel special and worthwhile. Show each person tremendous respect and consideration. Always be humble and apologize if you offend someone.
5. **Strong**—Be so steadfast, confident, loving, and calm that nothing can disturb your peace of mind and resolve.
6. **Compassionate**—Be patient, loving, and caring with yourself and others. Love people just as they are regardless of how unskillfully they may behave. Consistently keep in touch with others and be interested in them. Support and help them in overcoming their challenges and in being the best they can be. Express yourself honestly with kindness and concern.
7. **Opportunity-Oriented**—Let your fire for desire lead you to the opportunities you need to reach your goals and objectives, so you can make your dreams come true. Always look for and take advantage of opportunities every day to start and build fine, mutually beneficial relationships.

8. **Enthusiastic**—Be excited about what you are doing—and encourage others to be excited about what they're doing too. Regularly compliment people on their victories, large and small.

Thou Shalt:

9. **Forget the mistakes of the past**—Remember only the lessons. Press on with the belief that your past does not determine your future, unless you let it. Start each day anew with a positive attitude and great expectations.
10. **Thank everyone**—Always show appreciation to those who support and help you.

Remember that the key to your success is found in caring about others, as you help them overcome their challenges. Be a genuine friend to everyone with whom you work, associate, deal, or sell to, as well as others around you. You, too, can then become a master high-touch relationship builder.

Learn and sincerely apply The Ten Commandments of *High-Touch* Relationship Building. Living by them will help you win BIG with people so you can accomplish your goals and objectives—and make your dreams come true.

"*Meet new people and make more friends every time you have the opportunity. Always be nice, kind, and good to everyone, and a brighter world will open up to you.*"

—Tony Sciré

52 Tips to Help You Develop
the *Talent Of Networking Yourself*

*"Resolve attitude challenges creatively
and become the best you can be, while supporting
others in doing the same."*
—Tony Sciré—

Tip 1—History has demonstrated that the most success-ful people usually encountered challenging and even heart-breaking obstacles before they triumphed. They won because they refused to become discouraged by their defeats. They just kept on going—no matter what.

Tip 2—To make great first connections and lay the foun-dation for building high-touch relationships, implement the following:

- Give excellent eye contact.
- Assume a calm, relaxed state of breathing.
- Begin to create win-win scenarios.
- Focus on other people and how you can assist them in the kindest way possible with whatever you are doing.
- Increase your self-belief by telling yourself you can handle whatever obstacles you may encounter with your new relationships.

Create as many opportunities as you can to meet new people and develop relationships. Like anything else worth-while, this takes effort. But it's worth it. And if, for some reason, a relationship doesn't work out, that's okay. Be kind to that person anyway, and keep in touch—while continuing to meet and befriend others. Circumstances and people change.

Tip 3—Visit and connect with those you love. There's no excuse not to do it. Always do your best to blend it in with whatever else you are doing. For example, your employer, organization, or industry may offer an out-of-town continuing education or motivational seminar or convention. If you have friends or family in that area, go see them and rekindle your relationships. Who knows? You may be able to help them through what you are doing, or in some other way. And they may be able to help you, too, by giving you a referral, or doing something else special for you—now or later.

Tip 4—Work on developing a calm, loving, solid-as-a-rock presence. Always go for what you want, but be open to unexpected twists and turns along the way. Be flexible.

Tip 5—Be cheerful and maintain a lighthearted, uplifting outlook at all times. Don't take anything or anybody, especially yourself and your foibles, too seriously. Believe that life is an adventure!

Tip 6—Think kind thoughts and be kind. Think happy thoughts and be happy. Talk in an encouraging, positive way to everyone you know and meet, and you'll be encouraged too! Your positive thoughts and talk are essential to your happiness and well-being.

Tip 7—Help people feel great about themselves. Compliment others at every opportunity—say things you honestly mean that will build them up. Be appreciative of them and all they have to offer. Help others feel they are important and valuable. Be a generous, sincere compliment giver.

Tip 8—Create optimism in your heart and mind, and support others in doing the same. Use your people power to connect with others and reach your objectives, and teach others to do the same. Share what you are learning to educate, assist, and bolster others, so they can achieve their goals and, in turn, pass on what they learn from you.

Tip 9—Anticipate the best! Give yourself and others the benefit of the doubt. Look upon all people in a loving way as your sisters and brothers, regardless of what they say or do. As necessary, exercise extra patience and understanding.

Tip 10—Get fired up! Be passionate about who you are, what you are doing, and the difference you are making.

Tip 11—Create excitement! Pay attention to your heartfelt objectives, dreams, and goals. Know that, step by step, you can achieve them. Be a cheerleader for yourself and others. Celebrate your victories and those of others.

Tip 12—Believe with all your heart that you can become the person you want to be. All you need to do is keep growing and act as if you are that person today and every day—and so shall you become!

Tip 13—God Has Deputies:

> "[What about] men and women with clearer sight than some poor, benighted human who can seldom see the right? Don't you know my brothers! [and] sisters! [that] you will not serve God all right if you fail to lead those blind ones from their darkness to your light?"
>
> —*M. T. Sheahan*

Tip 14—A star is born. His mission is clear to me. Now is the hour when He gives me the power and shows me what I can be. A star is born to bring all the best out in me. I'm in a new generation with motivation. No hesitation is in me. The star that is born has entered the person you see. I know on this day we all will say, "The star that was born is me."

Tip 15—To Believe or Not to Believe:

"For those who believe, no explanation is necessary. For those who do not believe, no explanation is possible."
—*Father Samuel Constance*

Tip 16—The Magic Formula for Challenge Resolution:

"I keep six honest serving-men. They taught me all I know. Their names are What, Who, Why, When, Where, and How."

—*Rudyard Kipling*

Tip 17—Look to This Day!

"For it is life, the very life of life. In its brief course lie all the varieties and realities of your existence. The bliss of growth, the glory of action, the splendor of beauty. For yesterday is but a dream and tomorrow is only a vision, but today well lived makes every yesterday a dream of happiness and every tomorrow a vision of hope. Look well, therefore, to this day! Such is the salutation to the dawn."

—*Kalidasa, Dramatist*

Tip 18—Enjoy the Roses Today!

"All of us tend to put off living. We're dreaming of some magical rose garden over the horizon instead of enjoying the roses that are blooming outside our windows today!"

—*Dale Carnegie*

Tip 19—Live and do today. Yesterday is forever gone, while tomorrow is guaranteed to no one. Do the best you can today to live, grow, and help others.

Tip 20—Look at challenges as opportunities to take your relationships to new levels. There is always something good ahead when a challenge is handled with love and persistence, until it's resolved.

Tip 21—Remember, friends may come and go. However, enemies can accumulate. Therefore, make friends, not enemies! And be forgiving of yourself and others, as well as your environment. Never carry the burden of a grudge. It hurts you and makes you less happy.

Tip 22—Become knowledgeable about the facts, figures, features, and benefits of what you are offering or doing. Also learn about the wants and needs of the people to whom you are presenting. Do the best you can with the knowledge you have. If you don't know something, be humble enough to admit it. Then start learning about it—either from someone you know who has the information, or from another appropriate source.

Tip 23—Always keep your promises. Don't promise more than you can deliver. If you find you have fallen short, apologize, remedy the situation, or negotiate a new agreement.

Tip 24—"It's a wonderful life!" Be sure to share this joyful phrase with everyone. Always look for the good.

Tip 25—Remember, as someone said:

> "Success is getting up just one more time after you fall down!"
>
> —*Anonymous*

Tip 26—Support others in times of stress and crisis. Observe and read about those who do it well, and model yourself after them. Ask for help if you need it, for you are not alone. There are warmhearted people everywhere. The more warmhearted you are, the more you will attract such individuals into your life. Like attracts like.

Tip 27—How good you feel depends on the messages you give yourself every day. So wake up each day and pronounce, "I am making this day a great one!" Wake up each day and remember that you can start molding an exciting piece of your future with how you invest your time that day. Do productive things, day by day, to move yourself forward into your bright new goal-achieving future.

Tip 28—Discover who you really are and always be genuine. Give others the chance to get to know and love the real you. Do simple, kind things, and you'll feel good about yourself, while creating emotional connections. Etch love on people's hearts whenever you can and you will make life-long positive differences in their lives.

To observe someone's true character and level of compassion, watch how he or she treats somebody who can do absolutely nothing for him or her. A true sign of a compassionate person of admirable character is when that individual is kind to someone who can give nothing back, except maybe a smile and a thank you. Be sure you do the same.

Tip 29—I have never dug for gold. If I had, maybe I could tell you, from experience, how long it can take to reach the unknown. That is exactly what success is. It is an unknown quantity to all who are striving to achieve their goals. And that's where your faith really comes into play.

So, how long do you need to persevere to achieve your goals and objectives and make your dreams come true? Who knows? Just go forward in faith and keep going until you make them a reality! You can accomplish virtually anything you set your mind to, provided you consistently take appropriate action and don't give up.

Tip 30—There is one basic obstacle in life: the barrier of a poor attitude. If you say you can't do something, you're right—you can't. But when you say you *can* do something, you're also right—you can do it! So always say yes to a great, "can-do" attitude.

Tip 31—Nobody automatically rises to the top in business or in life. It takes hard work, and winners climb every inch of the way. But they don't just work hard. They also work smart. Keep climbing your way to the top of whatever "mountain" you are scaling. If you slip and fall, pick yourself up, dust yourself off, and keep on going. With persistence, you will overcome any challenges that may threaten to daunt you.

Tip 32—Being average is just not good enough. Besides, it's boring. Anybody can do that. To excel, you need to be great. Think great! Act great! Be great! Remember, being great is much better (and much more fun!) than being average.

Tip 33—Today, pick up the phone, call someone you've been ignoring, and share what you're doing. Start by saying, "Hello _____. This is _____." Go ahead—*you'll be glad you did!*

> "If you were going to die today and had only one phone call you could make, who would you call and what would you say? Why are you waiting?"
> —*Stephen Levine*

Tip 34—As long as you wake up each day and put a smile☺ on your face, you are doing something that can contribute to the human race. Smile☺ at someone today who you would not normally acknowledge. Look and smile☺ at all the people you know and meet, and watch as most of them smile☺ back at you. Be a people magnet by habitually sharing your appreciation of being alive with simple, sincere smiles☺☺.

Tip 35—Teach others to be happy by showing them how to have an attitude of gratitude for all their blessings. Encourage them to follow their hearts so they can add more joy to their lives. You may be surprised by the increased joy you'll feel as well.

Tip 36—Go ahead, step out, and talk to people you don't know. When you do, always remember to:

- Use common sense.
- Respect their feelings.
- Take an interest in what they have to say first.
- Make a positive difference in their lives.
- Create win-win experiences.

Tip 37—Correct people only in private, but never criticize or label them. Focus only on their unskillful behaviors and not on who they are. Kindly, but firmly, tell them how you felt when they did certain things. Save any counseling or advice for one-on-one sessions behind closed doors. Never put down or embarrass people. Imagine what it could be like to be in their positions. This helps you better understand and have empathy for them and their situations.

Tip 38—You were created to win, but you may have become conditioned to fail. You will succumb to your conditioning if you don't like or believe in yourself. But your internal voice *can* be your best friend—even if it's been your worst enemy in the past. Always say uplifting things to yourself. You simply cannot afford to think negatively. It will only drag you down and keep you from succeeding.

When you wake up each day, look in the mirror and acknowledge the following: "I have been created with a seed of greatness. I have been created to succeed, and I condition myself for that success. I can do anything I choose to do." Also say to yourself, "I like myself, and I can make a positive difference in at least one person's life today. I succeed every day in big and little ways."

Tip 39—Maintain a strong, positive attitude—especially as you work through challenges. Associate with supportive people and keep putting positive information into your brain. Be a consummate student of your job, business, or profession, or whatever else you are doing. Read from a positive, inspiring book at least 15 to 20 minutes a day, and listen to a motivational/educational tape.

Always listen to uplifting, informative tapes in your car to take advantage of commuting and other driving times. Always have a personal or business development book with you to read as you wait for people and appointments. Be an excellent example of someone who is constantly learning and growing. Take advantage of any continuing education programs available to you.

Tip 40—Totally focus on each person you're talking to, and listen intently to what is being said. Ask questions to clarify any misunderstandings, and treat him or her as you believe they want to be treated. This perspective allows you to listen with interest, sincerity, and empathy.

Tip 41—People generally know what they need to do. They may just need some encouragement, and to know you care enough to help them get moving. Invest your time in listening to others. It shows you care, and helps build their courage and self-respect. It may take them a while to believe you are concerned about them, because most people aren't. That's where your loving patience is needed. Give people time to grow to the point where they realize they are worthy of your kindnesses.

Tip 42—Appreciation and sensitivity are major qualities of a win-win state of mind. Always be generous with both. Thank someone in your support network by sending him or her a thank-you note or a little gift.

Tip 43—Do something nice every day to show you care about others. Regularly make a difference in their lives. One of the wonderful results you will experience is that you automatically make a difference in your own life when you touch the lives of others with your giving spirit.

Tip 44—Circulate to percolate at every opportunity. Continually expand and upgrade your sphere of influence. Get out there and network *everywhere* you go. Extend the hand of friendship. Find new ways to meet people by making every outing an adventure. Enjoy your life wherever you go!

Tip 45—Make some new choices to help yourself get out of your comfort or familiar zones. Do new things in your work, as well as personally and socially. Get excited about and take advantage of opportunities to face the unknown. Go ahead and take some chances. Get off any spinning-wheels-to-nowhere on which you may be stuck. Explore *new* territories and make *new* friends. Make discovering new places to meet new kinds of people one of your new high-priority activities.

Tip 46—Always communicate beyond superficial exchanges, that is, in more meaningful ways. Sincerely give of yourself. Those who want to communicate with you are likely to enjoy your company and have confidence in your ability to help them.

Tip 47—Increase your self-confidence. Join an association or organization of forward-thinking, supportive people who are looking to grow and network with others. This gives you the opportunity to meet people who can join with you to create the new results you want in your work and in your life. Help others do the same.

Tip 48—Expand your sphere of influence while being romantic with your spouse or that special someone. Make a concerted effort to regularly go out together in the evenings and on weekends and meet new people—attend local events, get ice cream cones, or just hold hands and take a walk. Always be aware and take advantage of any opportunities you have to connect with others. Nurture your special relationship by saying "I love you," at least once a day. Do little caring things. Show appreciation and consideration every day.

Tip 49—Build your fire for desire by focusing on your dreams, goals, and objectives. We were all created with the potential for success. However, no one was born successful. Most people we call gifted or talented got that way because of obsessive desire. Success comes only to those who cultivate their fire for desire. It drives them to develop skills and overcome the challenges they meet along the way toward accomplishing their goals.

Tip 50—Use *The Power of 2* business card technique. Ask the people you meet for two business cards. Tell them you'll keep one for your records and give the other one to someone you know or meet who could use what they have to offer. Then give two of your cards to them—one to keep for their records and one to give to someone who could benefit from meeting you.

Tip 51—Contacts can make you contracts. Meet new people and make more friends every time you have the opportunity. As appropriate, call them later and schedule presentations to share what you're doing or how you can help them. Remember, a major part of caring about others is in telling them what you know, are doing, or have to offer that could assist them.

Tip 52—Through your character, you reflect traits that make you special and unique. You are a person of value and have something to offer others that can make a positive difference in their lives. Always be *nice*, *kind*, and *good* to others and a brighter world will open up to you.

Now Go Share This Book with Others
Be a shining example—a beacon for others to follow. If you've found this book helpful and know some people who could benefit by reading it, be sure to tell them about it. You may even want to give a copy to a friend, or to someone you meet—and you'll make a new friend! They'll appreciate your thinking of them, and you'll feel good about doing it.

Let's make our relationships better than they have ever been before. Our workplaces, business environments, schools, and communities will then be kinder, gentler places to be.

In Conclusion
The best way to the top in your work and in life is to be *nice, kind,* and *good* to everyone you know and meet. Couple that with building high-touch relationships, and you'll be on your way to the happiness and success you desire. You simply can't do it alone. It all begins with *The Power of 2.*

The A to Z of *The Power of 2*

- **A**lways be friendly, say hello to, and talk with everyone you meet—and exchange two business cards with them.
- **B**e *nice, kind*, and *good* to others all the time, no matter how unskillfully they may behave.
- **C**all others to keep in touch—just to say hello and show you care.
- **D**on't quit when you get a no. Be more determined than ever.
- **E**nvision yourself successfully reaching your dream, goal, or objective.
- **F**orgive others and overlook the small, inconsequential stuff they do.
- **G**ive generously with an attitude of service rather than always looking to see, "What's in it for me?"
- **H**elp others whenever possible and teach them how to help themselves.
- **I**nvite others to have breakfast, lunch, dinner, or coffee with you to build and nurture more high-touch relationships.
- **J**ust be yourself when you are making presentations. Be knowledgeable, caring, and sincere. Share from the heart.
- **K**eep an open mind when meeting new people. Appreciate their differences, and always look for the good.
- **L**ove everyone for who they are—not what they have.
- **M**ake a positive difference in the lives of others whenever you can.
- **N**ever judge others. Look at your own behavior which may have contributed to any challenge you may be experiencing.
- **O**ffer your care and compassion to others, and invest time in supporting them.
- **P**lay a role in other people's successes.
- **Q**uiet your fear with prayer and overcome it with action.
- **R**emember birthdays and other special days.
- **S**mile☺ at those you don't know. That's where you'll find new friends.
- **T**ell the truth gently but firmly, no matter what you think others may want to hear.
- **U**nderstand other people's points of view. Listen and ask questions.
- **V**alue others' rights to live their lives in the ways they choose.
- **W**ake up every day with a grateful heart and the will to win.
- **EX**cite yourself when others in your arena succeed, and believe you can do it too. Model their accomplishments and winning ways.
- **Y**ield to others when they speak. Listen well and ask questions.
- **Z**oom in on the fine qualities and kindnesses of others.

In the Final Analysis

"**P**eople *are often unreasonable, illogical, and self-centered—forgive them anyway. If you are kind, people may accuse you of selfish, ulterior motives—be kind anyway. If you are successful, you will win some false friends and some true enemies—succeed anyway. If you are honest and frank, people may cheat you—be honest and frank anyway. What you spend years building, someone may destroy overnight—build anyway. If you find serenity and happiness, they may be jealous—be happy anyway. The good you do today, people will often forget tomorrow—do good anyway. Give the world the best you have, and it may never be enough—give the world the best you have anyway. You see, in the final analysis, it's all between you and God. It was never between you and them anyway. Even the least among you can do all that I have done and even greater things."*

—Mother Teresa

More *Power of 2?*

As the manuscript developed, it occurred to me that people would be interested in reading about others who have used the principles in *The Power of 2*. If you have a true story you'd like to share, send it to me, and I'll consider using it in my next book. It could be about yourself or others you know or have read about.

For example, how are you making your marriage or family life happier? What are you doing in your work, school, service organization, community, and other activities to create more caring relationships? Who has inspired you by his or her example—how and why? Who is the most loving, caring person you know, and why?

If you have or discover a *Power of 2* relationship-building story you think others would find valuable and enjoyable, in any area of life, I encourage you to send it to me! Be sure to provide as much information as you can about where you obtained your story. After you have completed it, fax, mail, or e-mail it to me at:

> *The Power of 2* Story Contributions
> Tony Sciré/Possibility Press
> One Oakglade Circle
> Hummelstown, PA 17036
>
> Fax: (717) 566-6423
> E-mail: posspress@aol.com

Who Is Tony Sciré?

Tony Sciré is an author, international businessman, corporate entertainer, keynote speaker, private client consultant, and executive coach. He is clearly one of today's most recognized and respected leaders and advocates of building friendships in work, as well as in personal life.

Tony will tell you, as he lights the stage with his *The Power of 2* presentation, that people prefer to work, associate, and do business with those they like, trust, and can call friends. He encourages people to be kinder, gentler, and more appreciative in their work and communities, as well as in other areas of life.

People are using more high-tech tools and changing the way they interact—communicating and buying on the Internet more than ever. Because of that, we all need to do something special to encourage others to meet, work, do business, and associate with us. Tony teaches us how! When he speaks, he relates to others incredibly well. His tremendous empathy for people and their challenges shines through.

Drawing on his 27-year career, which included sales, sales management, and being a vice president of a major international company, this New York-born professional loves people and makes friends wherever he goes. Tony has traveled the world, met with thousands of people, and is here to tell you this: "We all have feelings and long to have others care about us. Every one of us has been created for success, and engineered to do good and live a great life."

Making *The Power of 2* a real-life guide to building relationships was Tony's big dream, which was only strengthened by the tragedies of September 11, 2001. He is committed to expanding the *wonderful wave of kindness* that began that day. Because of those events, he is now doing so with more passion and love for others than ever before. He is also giving the net proceeds from this book to charity.

Tony lives in Florida with his wife, Gail, and his mother, Theresa. He and Gail have two adult children whom he loves more than life. Tony is currently working with a production company on a children's motivational movie. He can be reached via email at motivation@schmoozie.com and visited on the Web at www.schmoozie.com.

Share *The Power of 2* with Others

To purchase or order single copies
of the book, visit your local bookstore or
anywhere else books are sold.

For more information about how
Tony Sciré can help your company or
organization, call:
Gail Sciré, Personal Manager
1976 Timarron Way • Naples, FL 34109
Telephone: (941) 596-4905
motivation@schmoozie.com
www.schmoozie.com

Set the Stage for a Great Meeting with Tony Sciré, Corporate Entertainer and Author

Tony Is Available for:
Keynote Addresses • Private Client Seminars
Executive Coaching

Tony Offers Coaching for:
Sales Meetings • Client Presentations • Speech Improvement
Annual Meetings • Product Presentations • Executive Training
New-Hire Programs • Media Management • Video Conferences
Testimony Appearances • Witness Appearances
Special One-on-One Customer Programs

Quantity Sales of *The Power of 2*

The Power of 2 and all other *Possibility Press Books* are available at special quantity discounts when purchased in bulk by individuals, corporations, organizations, schools, and special interest groups. They may be used for education, motivation, sales promotions, premiums, fundraisers, reselling, and gifts. Call *Possibility Press* at (717) 566-0468 (9-5 ET/M-F), or email us at posspress@aol.com. Visit us on the web at www.possibilitypress.com, or at www.thepowerof2.us.